RADICAL
CARE

RADICAL CARE

Leading for Justice in Urban Schools

Rosa L. Rivera-McCutchen

FOREWORD BY Jamaal A. Bowman

TEACHERS COLLEGE PRESS

TEACHERS COLLEGE | COLUMBIA UNIVERSITY

NEW YORK AND LONDON

Published by Teachers College Press,® 1234 Amsterdam Avenue, New York, NY 10027

Library of Congress Cataloging-in-Publication Data

Names: Rivera-McCutchen, Rosa L., author.
Title: Radical care : leading for justice in urban schools / Rosa L.
   Rivera-McCutchen ; foreword by Jamaal A. Bowman.
Description: New York, NY : Teachers College Press, 2021. | Includes
   bibliographical references and index.
Identifiers: LCCN 2021012586 (print) | LCCN 2021012587 (ebook) | ISBN
   9780807765425 (paperback) | ISBN 9780807765432 (hardcover) | ISBN
   9780807779606 (ebook)
Subjects: LCSH: Education, Urban—Social aspects—United States. | Urban
   schools—United States. | Social justice and education—United States. |
   Educational equalization—United States.
Classification: LCC LC5131 .R58 2021 (print) | LCC LC5131 (ebook) | DDC
   370.9173/2—dc23
LC record available at https://lccn.loc.gov/2021012586
LC ebook record available at https://lccn.loc.gov/2021012587

ISBN 978-0-8077-6542-5 (paper)
ISBN 978-0-8077-6543-2 (hardcover)
ISBN 978-0-8077-7960-6 (ebook)

Printed on acid-free paper
Manufactured in the United States of America

To my Wings Academy students,
who first taught me the importance of radical care
before I fully understood what it was.

To Bronx school leaders N.M., S.M, and J.B.,
who showed me what it means to lead with radical care.

To my CUNY Lehman College students,
who are the future of radical care
in urban school leadership.

Contents

Foreword

Now more than ever, the world needs radical care. We have suffered through a collective trauma from a global pandemic that has killed over 2 million people and a recent attack on the United States Capitol by White nationalists. This was the first attack on the Capitol since the war of 1812. Hundreds of millions of people have fallen into poverty due to the pandemic, and the learning of millions of children has suffered due to closed schools and lack of access to remote learning opportunities.

Our schools will be essential spaces for collective healing, vigorous learning, and justice. The radical care framework, created by Rosa Rivera-McCutchen after years of research, articulates a vision for what leadership in our urban schools could and should be. Our urban schools serve as the heartbeat of our communities and act as catchalls for our communities' histories, triumphs, and trauma.

As we heal our children and move forward as a nation, we must embody radical care. I've had the privilege of working in urban schools for over 20 years, serving as a teacher, counselor, and middle school principal. I've learned alongside kids as young as 4 and as old as 19. What I have learned is that regardless of background or circumstances, children come to school ready, willing, and able to learn. They all want to be valued, make friends, and be successful. Rivera-McCutchen's framework provides a blueprint and pathway to their success.

So what is radical care? It is shaking the hands of and smiling at every child that comes into the school building. It is the occasional hug when a child needs it. It is listening and learning more from your children than you can possibly teach them. It is inspiring them socially, emotionally, physically, and cognitively. It is working collaboratively with parents and teachers who bring lived experiences to our classrooms that no textbook can provide. It is providing the resources and opportunities that our children need to grow and thrive.

But radical care is much more than that. The school leaders I most admire, and who have the best learning environments, adopt a clear and unapologetic antiracist disposition toward the work. School leaders who embody radical care must do their jobs daily with the understanding that Black, Latinx, and Indigenous people have been victims of historical terror and oppression, and continue to be victims of biased and racist policy. Therefore, radical care schools seek to heal these historical wounds, and empower students to be fully free—and fully human.

Rivera-McCutchen's framework also includes the understanding that learning is not simply an academic exercise, it is also relational. School leaders who embody radical care must build authentic relationships with parents, teachers, students, colleagues, and allies. These relationships are not transactional, which too often define America's market-based systems and institutions. Rather, radical care relationships are rooted in curiosity, equality, and growth. Authentic relationships also facilitate a school leader's ability to mitigate and manage risks. The status quo is not working for the majority of students. Therefore, the system must be critiqued and challenged to be better than it is. Many of our systems are designed based on the myth of White supremacy. As a result, the structures in our schools facilitate intergenerational harm for students of color. After the White nationalist attack on the Capitol, now more than ever we must use Rivera-McCutchen's framework to challenge these systems.

This book is important because it provides real-world examples of radical care in action. This book also reminds us that central to radical care is the radical certainty that we can make the world a magnificent place for everyone. We can and must build a new world that includes the ideas and talents of all children. This book helps us to radically imagine a world where every child has access to a healthy diet, dignified housing, spacious green play spaces, books, teachers, mentors, and tutors, and opportunities for their imaginations to be omnipotent and uninhibited. Rivera-McCutchen's framework provides a vision of something new and spectacular. Our children deserve nothing less—and we all deserve the privilege of having them lead the way.

—*Jamaal A. Bowman*

Acknowledgments

Writing can be a solitary and isolating act, but this book would not have been possible had I not had a village supporting me. My village includes a number of incredibly brilliant and strong women who have been in my personal and professional circles, with lots of overlap over the years and during the course of writing this book. Foremost among these is Carole Saltz, the former director of Teachers College Press, who walked up to me at a small conference we both attended and told me that I should write a book. Since that first conversation in 2015, we've broken bread several times, and all the while, Carole nudged and encouraged me, even after she retired. She first planted this idea in my head, and I owe her a deep debt of gratitude for helping me believe that this was possible.

Next are the scholar-sisters who have encouraged me, laughed with me, and inspired me. Long weekends and nights of talking, laughing, and plotting to transform the lives of Black and Latinx children alongside Soribel Genao, Sonya Douglas Horsford, Patrice McClellan, and Terri Watson fed my soul and energized me to do the work from the early days of my work in the field of educational leadership. Maria Hantzopoulos, Alia Tyner-Mullings, Melissa Martínez, Sharon Radd, and Nell Scharff Panero are also women whose intelligence and generosity have inspired and encouraged me over the years. I'm deeply grateful to have had the opportunity to collaborate with each of them. I owe a very special thanks to Sherry Deckman, who read early versions of this work and kept me accountable with perfectly timed "how's the writing going?" emails. While these women are all my colleagues in the academy, I am so blessed to also call them my friends.

I have also had a powerful village of sister-mamas and othermothers who have cheered me on and inspired me through our impassioned conversations and laughter, often with a glass of wine in hand. I honor the many Black and Latinx women in The Collective and my New Rochelle community who inspire me with their wisdom, sacrifice, and persistence on behalf of all Black and Latinx children in our "village." I also had an abundance of support from Coralie Gallet, Lucille Renwick, and

Rani Snyder, who each read an early draft of the manuscript and gave me feedback in the form of thoughtful questions that pushed my thinking, then continued to check in and encourage me. Anne De Nigris (aka "life coach") also gave me feedback on an early draft, then texted and checked in on me daily, her excitement for me and this book palpable. Each of these women celebrated me every step of the way. And a special thanks to Alene Morash who has always been on hand to offer encouragement, laughter, prayer, and a drink (and soup!).

My Lehman College School of Education and CLLSE department colleagues have given me a great deal of encouragement over the years, but there are several sister-colleagues who deserve special mention. Danielle Magaldi and Tamisha Bouknight were critical in helping me maintain my sanity, especially in the early years, through laughter, tears, and more laughter. Harriet "Niki" Fayne has also been a source of support since her arrival at Lehman. As I worked on the book, she happily took on the role of nudge and read through the manuscript in record time, giving me thoughtful feedback. My program colleague and friend Janet DeSimone has been one of my fiercest supporters and allies at Lehman since I arrived in 2010. Over the years, Janet protected my time, often taking on more than her share to give me space and time for my work. She's one of the most generous, thoughtful, and ethical people I know. Laura Roberts is another colleague whose big-hearted and thoughtful nature are qualities that make her such an incredible human being. I'm profoundly grateful for Janet and Laura's stellar leadership, their friendship, and their unique ability to make me cackle with laughter.

I also want to thank my line sisters—*The Talented Tenth,* DST, PB Sp. 95—for their support and encouragement. In the summer of 2019, as we waded in the beautiful Destin beach water for over an hour, we spoke our dreams out loud. We promised to help each other be accountable to ourselves and, true to us, we have done so with a good dose of laughter and prayer sprinkled throughout. These women are each power-houses in their own right, and I have been blessed to be a part of our sisterhood and journey since Spring 1995.

My two "ride or dies," Anne Marie Marshall and Bree Picower, have meant more to me over the years than words can adequately express. Anne Marie's telepathically timed text messages, inside jokes, shoulder-shaking laughter, and thoughtfulness have gotten me through many tough days over the years, and I'm so grateful for the day she joined the Lehman College family. Bree and I met on our first day as doctoral students at NYU in 2002 and we became instant besties after I asked her to give me her fried chicken skin, aghast that she would dare throw the best part away. Since then, she has been one of my fiercest champions, reminding me to value my own worth on a near daily basis, and always pushes me to "dig deeper." Bree's multiple close reads of each chapter draft, coupled with daily coaching, accountability, encouragement, and giggles were absolutely critical in helping me finish. I'm profoundly grateful to these two women.

My big sisters, Sonia Rivera Gomez and Anita (Katanga) Romero Warren, and my mother, Judy Rivera, are the women that I have spent my entire life emulating. Their passion for justice and humanity has been foundational to my formation as a woman, educator, researcher, mother, and human being. I hope I make them proud.

I next want to thank others in my life, both men and women, who have supported me along the way. First among these is Jamaal A. Bowman, who is not only my friend, but also my congressman. Our frequent conversations in-person, by phone, or via text over the past 10 years helped shape the radical care framework, and I'm grateful for his visionary leadership in schools and in the 116th Congress.

Aurora Chang provided valuable support at the prospectus stage of this book. William Waters, who has worked with me since my dissertation writing days, was also critical in helping me complete this book, even after an ongoing battle recovering from COVID-19, insisting that he wanted to be on "Team Rosa."

A huge thanks goes to my big brothers, Allan Warren and José Gómez, for their pride, encouragement, and good-natured teasing, as well as my countless nieces and nephews, cousins, aunts, and uncles, who teach me time and time again about the tested, yet unbreakable bonds of family. My father, Xavier Rivera, taught me this at an early age and continues to do so, despite the years that have passed since his death.

Finally, I want to thank my partner in love and life, Al, for his constant support and encouragement. As an educator, he embodies radical care, and his students are so lucky to have him in their corner. Last, but certainly not least, I want to thank our children Elliott (who contributed the cover art), Najah, and Anayah for being thoughtful, funny, silly, and visionary. *You* are why radical care is essential in schools.

Introduction

(Re)Conceptualizing Care in Urban Schools

Every morning, Byron Johnson,[1] a Black male principal, greets each one of his Black and Latinx middle school students as they walk into the Bronx school building. A pat on the back, a shake of the hand, a rough-but-loving hand on the head of the young men, Mr. Johnson makes clear that he cares for these students. He greets each child by name and asks how their loved ones are doing. There is a familial quality in these interactions, and it is evident that Mr. Johnson views the kids as if they are his own, looking out for their interests with fierce devotion and dedication.

When you ask educators why they chose their profession, among the reasons they share is that they "care about kids." As I frequently remind my graduate students in the leadership program at Lehman College, people generally don't enter the field of education for the glory, the pay, or even the summer vacations. Education is not as respected as it used to be, and most would agree that educators aren't paid what they deserve. As for the vacations, anyone who has stepped into a classroom for even one day can attest to the intense physical and mental strain involved in being in front of children all day. While the breaks are essential for restoration, ask any educator's kids or partners how their beloved spends their "breaks" and they will tell you that they spend much of their time grading or working to improve their practice and deepen their content knowledge for the upcoming year. So, when teachers and school leaders tell us that they entered the field of education because they "care" about kids, it makes perfect sense. You need to care about kids in order to want to teach them and certainly to want to lead in a school. We know that care is important in education.

Yet one of the challenges with the concept of care is that it means different things to different people, and how it's operationalized can often be paternalistic and superficial. In a course I teach on instructional supervision, the students in my classes are often reticent to directly address the

1

poor instruction they see when observing their peers in schools. When re-
luctantly sharing their critiques, they frequently frame poor performances
with the disclaimer of what a good person the teacher is or they excuse
the performance because the teacher was having an off day. They do this
because they care about their colleagues and want to protect them. Other
times, my students will talk about the communities their schools serve as
being deficient and dangerous and, because they care about the children
in their schools, my leadership students frequently talk about themselves
as saviors for the children and the communities they serve. These two
examples of how aspiring leaders frequently talk about, and likely enact,
care demonstrates how damaging superficial caring can be to students,
communities, and peers.

Each of these examples highlight forms of what I call *limiting care,*
a term I return to throughout the book, because although it is frequently well-meaning, at its core it does more harm than good. The person
practicing limiting care ignores structural inequities that can only be dismantled through deep and sustained work. However, I prefer to use the
term limiting care because it explicitly calls out the long-term harmful
effects of this form of care. It is too frequently characterized by pity and
excuse-making made ostensibly in the service of children. That is, educators will tend to focus on what's standing in the way of the child being
successful and, in the interest of supporting them, mistakenly make it
easier for students to be "successful" by asking students to do less or accept mediocrity. Scholars René Antrop-González and Anthony De Jesús
(2006) have referred to this as "*ay bendito,*" or "blessed be," which refers
to a Puerto Rican and other Latinx expression of empathy. More recently,
Miguel Cardona, President Joseph Biden's nominee for U.S. Secretary
of Education, referred to educators' pity for students as the "ay bendito
effect" (Education Secretary Confirmation Hearing, 2021). This form of
limiting care is actually the stuff of lowered expectations. Other forms of
limiting care are characterized by an unwillingness to acknowledge race
and difference. Without engaging with race and racism, the conditions of
institutional and systemic racism cannot be disrupted; this form of limiting care again inhibits structural transformation that changes the material
conditions of Black and Latinx communities.

Over the years, as I've worked and studied in and with Bronx schools
as a professor of education, what I've come to learn is that limiting care is
deeply problematic and insufficient. What we need in schools, particularly
in the kinds of schools that serve Black and Latinx students, is something
that I call *radical care*—the kind of care demonstrated by principal Byron
Johnson in the above vignette.

RADICAL CARE

I first started to consider the power of the word *radical* in conjunction with the concept of care, which I've studied for years, just after the 2016 presidential election, when a series of essays was published in *The New Yorker*. Novelist Junot Díaz (2016),[2] one of the featured authors, penned an essay in which he cited philosopher Jonathan Lear and called for *radical* hope. Díaz argued that it,

> is not so much something you have but something you practice; it demands flexibility, openness, and what Lear describes as "imaginative excellence." Radical hope is our best weapon against despair, even when despair seems justifiable; it makes survival on the end of your world possible. (2016, para. 8)

The term *radical* invokes possibility with urgency and passion, which are essential when thinking about how to improve schools in communities that have historically been neglected. Radical hope, as described by Díaz, compels us to move away from a complacent acceptance of what is and imagine an alternative reality for schooling. We need to push past a tendency to despair when thinking about urban education and consider what is radically possible. Radical hope, coupled with care, can have a tremendous impact on communities that need leaders to act out of a sense of urgency *and* deep affection for the students and families they serve.

Radical care goes beyond structural changes, which is where most school reform tends to happen. Decreasing school size or curricular revision, for example, both common structural reform strategies, are superficial and insufficient reforms if they are not coupled with a radical care framework. Transforming structures is important but without spending enough time thinking about the underlying ethic that is driving the changes, we run the risk of simply reproducing the same inequities but with a different twist. This is why I argue in this book that radical care needs to be at the center of school reform.

In my 20 years of experience working in and researching urban schools, I have come to understand that radical caring is central to the work of successful school leadership. This book explicitly outlines a conceptualization of a radical care framework that includes five components:

- Adopting an antiracist stance
- Cultivating authentic relationships
- Believing in students' and teachers' capacity for excellence

- Leveraging power strategically
- Embracing a spirit of radical hope

At the heart of radical care is antiracist leadership, which provides a lens for understanding how structural racism shapes and constrains the schooling experiences of Black and Latinx students. Antiracist practices lay a foundation for school leaders to cultivate deeply authentic relationships between the educators, students, and family members, placing value in their experiences and knowledge. Through radical care, leaders can create an expectation that students and teachers have the capacity to excel while providing both with appropriate supports and opportunities for growth. School leaders who practice radical care also recognize that their positional authority grants them power to advocate for structural change in strategic ways. With a spirit of radical hope and an urgent visionary mindset, leaders can thoughtfully engage in the work of creating the schools that Black and Latinx students deserve.

A CONTINUUM OF CARE

A good deal of research has focused on the need for caring in schools and has informed my own conceptualization of radical care. Well-known for her work on caring in education, Nel Noddings (2005) argues that caring is a relational dynamic. In order for caring to truly be present, Noddings argues, the person who is cared for must receive and be open to the caring that is offered by another person. The exchange cannot be described as "care" if the relational aspects are not present. That is to say, there needs to be mutuality and reciprocity in order for it to be described as a caring relationship.

Noddings's conceptualization is helpful in beginning to distinguish pity from care, but her framing does not go far enough in describing the essential qualities required in order for students, particularly marginalized ones, to feel truly cared for. What is missing is an explicit discussion of how race and deficit perspectives inform educators' expressions of care that often resemble pity, or limiting care. To build on her work, other scholars have advocated for *authentic* care, where educators are interested in the well-being of the student holistically (Valenzuela, 1999), or *critical* care where the relationships are informed by the sociopolitical and historical forces that have shaped and limited access to high-quality schooling for marginalized youth (Antrop-González & De Jesús, 2006; Rivera-McCutchen, 2012; Rolón-Dow, 2005).

Angela Valenzuela (1999) extended caring theory in her description of the schooling experiences of United States–born and immigrant Mexican youth, differentiating between aesthetic and authentic care. Drawing from her seminal ethnographic case study, *Subtractive Schooling,* Valenzuela described one Houston, Texas, high school as being subtractive, emphasizing an aesthetic form of caring, consequently subtracting the inherent cultural wealth of students. *Aesthetic care* is superficial in that it involves a hyperfocus on academic achievement and other kinds of performative behaviors related solely to school outcomes. On the contrary, Valenzuela argues, authentic care is grounded in seeing the whole student and their inherent knowledge and promise. Yet, while authentic care is essential, Valenzuela asserts that it must be accompanied by an acknowledgment and action around the politics of power and its impact on the schooling of children who have historically been oppressed.

Other scholars (see Antrop-González, 2011; Antrop-González & De Jesús, 2006; Rolón-Dow, 2005) have extended the concept of caring, theorizing that critical care should adopt a more equity-focused stance. They draw upon critical race theory to integrate considerations of race into the act of caring, even more explicitly than the caring that Valenzuela described. Antrop-González and De Jesús (2006) have argued that critical caring in schools is enacted through explicit organization of the formal and informal structures of schooling and curricula that are responsive to race and ethnicity. In their studies of two Latinx-based community schools, they highlight the potential of schools that are organized along the principles of critical care. Extending prior research in this area, Antrop-González and De Jesús's framework explicitly embeds high academic expectations along with strong teacher–student interpersonal relationships while also privileging the students' and communities' cultural knowledge.

Drawing from Antrop-González and De Jesús's (2006) and Rivera-McCutchen's (2012) research, Curry's (2016) anthropological study of a high school rite of passage program for Latinx students exemplified what she called "authentic *cariño*" (Spanish for "affection"), a tripartite concept that incorporates critical caring, as well as familial and intellectual caring. Like others, Curry's conceptualization of caring adopts a critical stance that is responsive to the historical and sociopolitical factors that impact communities of color. However, she adds to this framework by incorporating a nurturing element that resembles familial relationships whereby teachers care about the moral, social, and personal development of their students. Curry builds on the concept of critical care by explicitly calling for "intellectual *cariño*," which she describes as rigorous curricula coupled with necessary supports to help students achieve real academic success that will lead to fulfillment in life beyond school.

While these dominant theories of care are frequently invoked in terms of schooling, they are often limited to capturing the ethic of the teachers, largely leaving the principals and other leaders out of the discussion. Yet some leadership research has attempted to bridge this gap and has highlighted the importance of caring relationships and environments among principals and other leaders (Louis et al., 2016; Marshall et al., 1996). In particular, caring leadership is noted as being especially important in schools with large concentrations of students who have been historically and systematically marginalized (Tichnor-Wagner & Allen, 2016).

Similar to teacher research literature, there is an emerging, more critical strand of research in leadership that underscores the power of critical care (Bass, 2012), particularly among Black educators. Building on womanist forms of caring, which is rooted in a maternal instinct and a sense of collective responsibility for children (Beauboeuf-Lafantant, 2002; Price, 2009), other scholars in the field of educational leadership highlight examples of practitioners whose leadership is firmly rooted in a tradition of critical care that is connected to the community in ways that extend beyond superficial forms of caring (see Bass, 2012, 2016; McClellan, 2020; Wilson, 2016; Witherspoon & Arnold, 2010). Critical care in school leadership, as used by these authors, is described as going beyond traditional conceptions of care relating to trust and relationship building and is grounded in confronting and dismantling historically inequitable systems in schooling (Rivera-McCutchen, 2019, 2021; Wilson, 2016). In this book, I build on the prior research and argue that radical care is an essential framework for effective leadership practices.

URBAN SCHOOLS

Throughout this book, I use the term *urban* to describe the context of my work. However, I recognize that this word is loaded because it is a broad term often used pejoratively as a proxy to describe "bad" neighborhoods and people in cities, or as an inaccurate way of describing a mythical monolithic "Black" culture (Miller et al., 2011). The way I am using the term describes a city context, much like the areas where the majority of my research, teaching, and activism for more than 20 years has been situated. However, when I talk about radical care in urban schools, I am making a distinction between urban schools that serve predominantly affluent White students and schools serving historically underserved low-income Black and Latinx communities.

I also take certain liberties with the term *urban* and extend these geographic boundaries somewhat to include inner-ring suburban communities that resemble their city neighbors (Hanlon, 2009; Terbeck, 2020). While the inner-ring school systems generally have more resources than their metropolitan counterparts, as Lewis-McCoy's (2014) research has shown, Black and Latinx families within these communities often have limited access to those resources, much like their counterparts in larger cities. I therefore use the term *urban* to describe both the metropolitan and suburban communities where Black and Latinx students are in the majority.

Despite the systemic oppression facing members of the communities I refer to in this book, these communities are also inherently rich with familial, cultural, aspirational, and other forms of cultural wealth (Yosso, 2005). Radical care aims to address systemic oppression within these spaces and improve the conditions of schooling for historically oppressed students building on existing community cultural wealth.

THE CASE FOR RADICAL CARE

Despite several reauthorizations of the 1965 Elementary and Secondary Education Act (ESEA) over the last several decades, a 2018 report released by the U.S. Commission on Civil Rights (USCCR) noted that school districts that serve the most disadvantaged student populations are generally lagging in terms of providing equal access to high-quality educational experiences when compared to their counterpart schools serving more affluent and White communities. The report found that material resources, including facilities and technology, are frequently substandard and can exacerbate inequities. Not surprisingly, the report highlighted how educational inequality is inextricably linked to housing inequality, further underscoring the need to dismantle systems of oppression if we are to improve educational outcomes for Black and Latinx communities. Based on the overwhelming evidence that educational opportunities are persistently unequal and inequitable, the USCCR report urged Congress to act to define access to a high-quality public education as a federal right. Leaders who practice radical care understand that this work goes beyond affectionate relationships with students, to recognizing the need to address the kind of persistent inequality highlighted in the USCCR report.

USCCR's findings echo earlier studies that also point to the impact of opportunity gaps on Black (Education Trust, 2014a) and Latinx students' (Education Trust, 2014b) long-term academic outcomes when compared to their White counterparts. For example, Black and Latinx students have fewer opportunities to take advanced placement courses or enroll in courses required for college readiness. While the percentages of Black and Latinx students enrolling in college is on the rise, they are more likely than their White peers to enroll in for-profit colleges, rather than 2- or 4-year nonprofit institutions of higher education. Furthermore, although Black and Latinx students have demonstrated important gains in achievement on the National Assessment of Educational Progress (NAEP) reading and math assessments, in many school districts, they still lag behind their White peers on the same assessments (Education Trust, 2014a, 2014b).

There is likely no greater example of the disparities described by the USCCR than in New York, where school segregation is the worst in the country (Kuscera & Orfield, 2014), and in New York City, in particular, which is one of the drivers of the state's abysmal ranking. Years ago, Jonathan Kozol (1991, 2005) documented the "savage inequalities" in the Bronx, NY, schools and other low-income and racially segregated communities; over time, these patterns have persisted in creating predictably unequal schools for marginalized Black and Latinx youth in New York City (Hannah-Jones, 2016) despite the engaged activism of grassroots community organizations like Mothers on the Move (Mediratta & Karp, 2003), Northwest Bronx Community and Clergy Coalition, and others across the country (Warren & Mapp, 2011). These disparities are not merely the result of poorly executed policies; rather, they are the byproducts of the structural racism that has systematically denied Black and Latinx students access to opportunities in schools (Horsford, 2011; Ladson-Billings, 2006; Ladson-Billings & Tate, 1995). Failing to acknowledge structural racism in efforts to improve schools essentially puts the responsibility on students and their families, without providing the institutional or material conditions required for success. This is limiting care, because it assumes a "bootstrap" mentality that ignores how the system is reproducing educational oppression.

A related issue that has compounded inequitable schooling outcomes are the high-stakes accountability mandates ushered in by the passage of the No Child Left Behind Act (NCLB), the 2001 reauthorization of ESEA. While accountability policies may intend to shrink achievement gaps, the results often yield the opposite outcomes (Au, 2011). Though NCLB compelled school districts to disaggregate assessment data thereby highlighting stark disparities in outcomes among the most marginalized student populations, the rigid and punitive accountability mandates generally exacerbated the gaps (Darling-Hammond, 2010; McNeil et al., 2008; Vasquez Heilig & Darling-Hammond, 2008). As testing mandates intensified, schools serving low-income Black and Latinx students responded by increasing their emphasis on teaching to the test and reducing curricular offerings on nontested content areas (Graham et al., 2013; Smith, 2000). Already scarce resources for arts education and other content areas that were not tested were redirected to English language arts and math, where the majority of high-stakes tests were administered (Volger, 2003), having the effect of deepening inequities. Absent a radical care mindset in which school leaders can understand how the testing policies are part of a larger system of oppression, the fundamental conditions that reproduce inequality are ignored. School leaders have overemphasized test preparation rather than working to dismantle the systemic oppression that undergirds the testing industry.

Another example of how a lack of radical care leadership can undermine the successful transformation of schools is the New Century High School Initiative funded in the early 2000s in large part by the Gates Foundation. Inspired by Deborah Meier's Central Park East Secondary School, millions of dollars were used to close down comprehensive high schools across the country, many of them in New York City, and specifically in the Bronx. Across New York City, nearly 200 new small schools were established. The basic idea was that smaller schools would lead to greater personalization and better learning outcomes. While some of the schools have had success (Bloom et al., 2010), many of them have struggled with the same challenges as the schools they replaced (Kolodner, 2015). Absent radical care leadership, many have closed, leaving in their wake communities of teachers, families, and children left behind to pick up the pieces, yet again.

Small schools, per these reform efforts, were supposed to be the panacea, solving all of the problems of failing urban schools. The theory of change was that by limiting the size of the schools and creating smaller learning environments, teachers would know their students better and would more effectively reach kids who were struggling. Likewise, there was a belief that smaller staffs would lead to greater communication and collaboration among the educators. On its face, these are reasonable assumptions. Yet the path to success proved to be more complex and to require more than simply downsizing. As Meier (2003), Michelle Fine (2005), and others (Hantzopoulos & Tyner-Mullings, 2012) have cautioned repeatedly, "small" is a condition for other kinds of school improvement to take root; it is not the reform in and of itself. While shifts in curriculum, instruction, and assessment are essential, without radical care, these changes do little to disrupt systemic oppression.

Radical care, in particular because it addresses structural oppression and strategically leveraging power and relationships, is central to the work of improving urban schools and provides powerful leverage for creating curricular, instructional, and assessment transformation. Absent this, a small school runs the risk of becoming what scholar Michelle Fine has described as a "large high school in [disguise]" (2005, p. 11), where students are not known or cared for. *Radical Care: Leading for Justice in Urban Schools* addresses a gap in how we talk about and conceptualize care, and I argue that an ethic of radical care in school leadership is essential for improving educational outcomes for students who have been systematically denied access to opportunity.

ARRIVING AT RADICAL CARE

I am Puerto Rican and a first-generation college graduate. I grew up in a predominantly working-class Black, tight-knit community in Queens, New York, where the neighbors were part of our extended family. Like my parents before me, I attended NYC public schools from kindergarten through 12th grade. My father had been a police officer, but he retired shortly after I was born when he was diagnosed with an aggressive form of multiple sclerosis. My mother was a homemaker and deeply involved in community activism. My two sisters and I grew up on a very fixed income that consisted solely of my father's Social Security and disability benefits. Despite a lack of resources for summer camps or enrichment programs, my mother was strategic and knew how to advocate on behalf of her kids. When it came time for me to go to high school, through her network of other moms in the community, she was able to successfully get me admission into what we would now call a STEM program. That access afforded me some opportunities that I might not have had if I had attended my locally zoned high school.

I followed my middle sister to the University of Rochester where I earned my bachelor's degree in political science and then my master's degree in secondary social studies education. The University of Rochester is a private, predominantly White institution in upstate New York, and I experienced quite a shock when I arrived, both culturally and academically. While I had been near the top of my graduating class at Jamaica High School, then a school of roughly 2,000 kids, I struggled in college. In particular, the writing projects I was assigned were hard. In high school, I had never been asked to write anything more than a 2-page handwritten essay. There were no research projects and revisions, and certainly there were no 5-, 10-, 15-, or 20-page typed papers. I constantly found it difficult to meet the minimum page requirements on my papers, though not for a lack of effort. It wasn't until my junior year that a professor in a research seminar sat me down and explained that the term paper I was struggling to write lacked a thesis. As I looked back at my other papers, I realized that this was the underlying problem for me. The mechanics of writing a cogent paper eluded me, and yet I generally earned an A or A- in my college courses. My ideas were sound, and professors, mostly White, typically gave me the benefit of the doubt. These educators may have understood their actions to be caring, but in fact their actions more closely resembled pity and lowered expectations, qualities of limiting care.

As I entered my master's degree program in secondary social studies education, I began to reflect on what I had not been taught in my K–12 years. I began to understand that the limited expectations and deficit perspectives held of me and my classmates had hindered me academically during my college years, particularly in the area of writing. My college professors, who may have thought they were demonstrating care, also held limiting beliefs about my abilities that ultimately impeded my learning. In fact, they were enacting a form of limiting care; by not requiring the highest academic standards of me, coupled with support, their form of caring did little more than guarantee that I was underprepared.

I went on to start my career in education as a humanities high school teacher in the Bronx, which was also quite a shock. I was astounded by how my 9th-grade students had been so utterly undereducated prior to arriving in high school. When my colleagues and I would encounter a student who could write in complete sentences and write a decent essay, we were effusive in our praise and declared them college ready. Not surprisingly, far too many of these students went off to college only to leave without graduating, feeling defeated by the academic rigors, let alone the cultural shock. While I loved my students and developed deep relationships with them over the years, in retrospect, I realize I had not practiced radical care because I did not situate what was happening in my classrooms within broader structural inequities and systemic racism. I unconsciously lowered my expectations about what they could accomplish because their life circumstances were challenging. In so doing, I also lowered expectations for what I should and could accomplish with students. By failing to demand and expect excellence of myself and my students, I was complicit in their miseducation, just as my teachers had been complicit in mine.

When I began my doctoral studies at NYU years later, I had two burning questions: First, what are the conditions of schooling that contribute to a reproductive cycle that *under*educates kids that look like me? And more importantly, I wondered what do the schools where academic success and caring relationships are both present and who served students similar to the ones I had in the Bronx do differently? These questions have guided my research over the years and have informed my understanding of the need for radical care in urban school leadership.

ORGANIZATION OF THE BOOK

This book is organized to provide the reader with a deep understanding of each of the five components of a radical care framework, while integrating relevant research and providing vignettes from my research and experiences over the years to illustrate the embodiment of the component. These vignettes exemplify each of the components, demonstrating practical strategies for leading with radical care (see the Appendix for descriptions of the schools I refer to in this book where radical care is practiced). I want to emphasize that while adopting an antiracist mindset is at the core of radical care in leadership, this framework should be understood as holistic and synergistic. I tease it apart for the purpose of clarity, but in practice, these elements should be viewed as part of a larger whole and operating in concert with each other. You will see hints of this throughout the book as I unpack the framework.

Chapter 1 delves into the first component, adopting an antiracist stance, providing the reader with an overview of critical race theory (Bell, 1992; Delgado & Stefancic, 2017). I start with race because it is fundamentally integral to the challenges facing urban schooling and attempts at reform. I argue that engaging effectively in urban school leadership requires knowledge about the legacy of racism and its impact on the conditions of urban schooling today (Ladson-Billings, 1998; Ladson-Billings & Tate, 1995). If school leaders are blind to this legacy, they cannot connect the dots to understand that the very conditions of urban schools are directly linked to the systemic practices of limiting opportunities for children of color (Ladson-Billings, 2006). If leaders have an ahistorical and colorblind lens, they run the risk of blaming the children they serve for the gaps rather than focusing on dismantling structures that predict academic failure. I highlight the importance of leadership practices that are grounded foremost in an awareness of the history of a community, the sociopolitical processes that have a profound impact on how schools work, and a commitment to action that is grounded in racial justice. Race and racism are topics that make people uncomfortable; yet, without confronting them, radical care cannot exist.

In Chapter 2, I focus on the second component of radical care, the importance of cultivating authentic relationships that are centered on the student as a whole person, and go beyond acknowledging solely their academic identities. Unlike aesthetic care, where the primary emphasis is on academic achievement (Valenzuela, 1999), radical care demands that authentic relationships be central to the academic endeavor. Absent these kinds of connections, schools tend to focus solely on academic success and test scores, ignoring the other needs of the children they serve. Without taking into account the needs of the child as a whole, schools cannot help them improve academically. School leaders must model and guide teachers and staff in forming these authentic relationships that are concerned with students' socioemotional well-being, their families' well-being, and an acknowledgment and celebration of the students' inherent value. Further, as I highlight through vignettes, these relationships are informed by an acute awareness of racism, the politics of power, and its impact on the schooling of children who have historically been oppressed.

While building authentic relationships can lead to students having a greater sense of belonging and increased academic success, it must be coupled with a third component, a belief in students' and teachers' capacity to be excellent. In Chapter 3, I discuss how leaders whose practices are grounded in an ethic of radical care are aware that low expectations pervasive in many urban schools serving predominantly Black and Latinx children are often informed and shaped by racism. They understand that lowered expectations for students in the short-term can severely limit students' opportunities in the long-term (Bromberg & Theokas, 2013; Wildhagen, 2012). Moreover, leading with radical care demands that explicit and honest conversations about low expectations be an integral part of curriculum and instruction planning. Teachers are central to the work of radical caring in schools, and so leaders must explicitly set high expectations for them. Leading with radical care requires pushing teachers to be reflective about the rigor in their teaching practices. Furthermore, practices that are lacking in rigor must be publicly surfaced and interrogated.

In Chapter 4, I discuss the fourth component, leveraging power strategically, which focuses specifically on the importance of the principal as a change agent who navigates the external context, while skillfully leading within the school community (Khalifa, 2012; Lomotey, 1993). Principals whose leadership is grounded in an ethic of radical care thoughtfully examine externally imposed policies and practices to determine if their impact will cause their students harm. Through careful cultivation of a broad and diverse base of allies, these leaders carefully evaluate policies and, if noncompliance is in order, they decide when and how to resist. Illustrating this element through vignettes of urban school leaders, this chapter highlights the importance of leaders engaging in strategic and active resistance in order to protect the children and the communities they serve.

In Chapter 5, I argue that the fifth component, embracing a spirit of radical hope despite the trauma and hardship that many communities face, is essential to the work of radical care in leadership. Many urban schools are underresourced, as are the communities they serve. The challenges, at times, seem insurmountable; it is essential, then, that school leaders maintain a level of intensely radical hope if they are to effectively lead. This quality allows the school leaders to energize themselves and the communities they lead. It empowers them to believe that change and betterment are possible, and that the risks they take to lead their school communities will lead to improved outcomes for the students they serve. It is, as Díaz described, pushing past despair and embracing imaginative excellence.

In the concluding chapter, I provide an overview of the five components of radical care and give an example of how the components work in unison. In addition, the chapter offers recommendations for how schools of education that are preparing school leaders might also teach and use the framework in their work. Radical care is a way of leading that moves beyond the individual circumstances and conditions of schooling and works to create meaningful structural changes in urban schools. This book represents what is possible. It is an amalgam of leadership practices that I've witnessed over the years in various spaces. It is aspirational and, yes, it's a tall order. But I've seen enough in my years in the field of education to believe that radical care is achievable.

CHAPTER 1

Component 1
Adopting an Antiracist Stance

A veteran White teacher at Evergreen High School, who was generally known among colleagues for his covertly and overtly racist rhetoric, angrily lectured his Black and Latinx students about poor academic outcomes among students of color. He yelled at his class of 9th-graders, "This is why you people don't graduate from high school! If I were teaching in an all-White school, I wouldn't have this problem!" The students, who felt hurt and angered by the comments, went to the principal, Brendan Mazino, with their complaints and asked him how they could be expected to learn if their own teacher freely spewed racist statements and doubted their academic abilities. Mazino met with the teacher in private, but no other action was taken.

At the core of radical care in leadership is antiracism, and I highlight the example above as a way to underscore what schooling looks like when it is absent. Several teachers of color in the school reported this situation to me after being deeply disturbed by what they perceived to be a trend in the school. In this situation, not only is there a veteran teacher who has a history of expressing racist views with impunity, but the school leader's inaction in this case makes him equally complicit in fostering a racist climate. As a result, the students of color in the teacher's class are harmed, and the harm seeps out and poisons the environment for all other students, educators, and staff of color in the school (Kohli, 2018).

Rather than allow a hostile racial environment to flourish, leaders who practice radical care explicitly confront racism in ways that demonstrate their alignment and support of Black and Latinx people, and other people of color. By failing to support the students in the vignette shared above, the principal sent a message to all in the school that the humanity of Black and Latinx people was not valued. The principal's failure to act explicitly in this moment conveyed to those individuals that they would not find recourse in appealing to the leadership. And by failing to act forcefully and unapologetically, it set the stage for other incidents, whether perpetrated by this teacher or others.

The first component of radical care is adopting an antiracist stance, which is a mindset that is coupled with action. If the principal in this vignette were practicing radical care, I would argue that this incident might not have happened in the first place. That is to say, the leader would have worked to cultivate a culture and climate that explicitly rejected White supremacy and racial oppression. This would be evident in the ongoing professional learning that explicitly focused on understanding and dismantling racial oppression. Antiracist curricula would be well-established and integrated in the school's course offerings. Images throughout the building would have affirmed the humanity of Black and Latinx students and other students of color. In other words, it would be understood that the views expressed by the teacher were misaligned with the antiracist values of the school community.

On the other hand, if this incident were to still happen in a school where radical care was practiced, the leaders would first meet with the teacher directly and, shortly thereafter, provide a forum for the school community to explicitly address the racist rhetoric, embracing this as a critical opportunity to deepen the school's commitment to antiracism. The school leader might also work in partnership with others within the school community, including other educators, students, and parents, to review existing processes and protocols to ensure that antiracist and antioppressive practices are deeply embedded within the school's systems. This might include reassessing hiring and teacher evaluation practices to ensure that these procedures are aligned with antiracist values.

Enacting the first component of radical care, adopting an antiracist stance, goes beyond reading a book about race. Instead, school leaders would engage in the continuous processes of understanding structural racism and they would unpack the commonly used "Four Is of oppression and advantage" framework: ideological, institutional, interpersonal, and internalized.[1] Using radical care to advance an antiracist climate would involve ongoing analysis and active disruption of teaching and curricular practices that reinforce and prop up racism (Picower, 2021). This chapter illuminates how adopting an antiracist stance is critical to leading with radical care.

WHAT DOES IT MEAN TO ADOPT AN ANTIRACIST STANCE?

Employing a radical care framework for adopting an antiracist stance requires an active and deeply conscious commitment to examine racism in all forms and spaces. This first component of radical care is characterized by a deep examination of the self and extends to an examination of systemic and institutional oppression. School leaders, like the rest of us, have grown up in a racist society and they have not been immunized from the constant reminders regarding the superiority and normalcy of Whiteness (Billings, 2016; Picower, 2012). Because they have seen the pervasive positive reflections of Whiteness in the media, pop culture, literature, and other outlets, school leaders adopting an antiracist stance have to work to undo that messaging. This begins with leaders taking the initiative to engage in the hard work of learning about the history of race and racism and thoughtfully analyzing how systems work to reproduce racism.

For White leaders, antiracism means first examining their own internalized racial superiority and how it informs their leadership practices and choices. This includes considering how they make decisions about who they invite to engage in decisionmaking processes, such as building leadership teams. It can also include thoughtful consideration of how staff meetings are organized to privilege White voices over those of Black and Latinx people, and other people of color. Their choices about the teachers whose opinions are elevated within the various institutional spaces can reflect their internalized racial superiority, even if it is unconscious.

Further, White leaders who want to adopt an antiracist stance must confront their own complicity in maintaining racism in their everyday interactions but also in the systems and institutions where they have racial privilege. Leaders who work to be antiracists do not burden people of color on their staff with the expectations that they should share antiracism resources or explain how White colleagues' actions may be racist (DiAngelo, 2018; Kendi, 2017). Using radical care to adopt an antiracist stance means that leaders must be allies alongside people of color, using their racial privilege as leverage to engage other White people in conversations and to enter into spaces that might not be easily accessible, either physically or emotionally, to people of color. Finally, it means engaging and re-engaging in self-reflection about how they work are reifying racist structures.

Similar to White people, leaders of color have also been bombarded with negative images about Black and Latinx people, and other people of color. They have learned from a very young age that Whiteness is the desirable norm, while anything other is undesirable. Therefore, for leaders of color, adopting an antiracist stance also begins with deep self-reflection about the history of race and racism, and the impact it has had on developing internalized oppressions and feelings of inferiority (Woodson, 1933/1977). Like White people, antiracism for people of color also involves a critical analysis of institutional, systemic, and structural racism and a rejection of the notion of a race-neutral meritocracy and how it is manifested in the ways systems are organized. It requires an analysis of how systems work to maintain racial inequality (Bonilla-Silva, 2017; Kendi, 2017; Wilkerson, 2020).

School leaders must adopt an unwavering and unrelenting focus on antiracism in order to address issues of racial injustice; additionally, they should be pushing all those around them to similarly engage in understanding race and racism. Although many would argue that focusing on race creates more discord, such as inflamed dialogue and perhaps an increase in protests, the truth is that communities of color have always been aware of race and the impact of racism on their daily lives. The absence of a focus on race and racism does not mean that it hasn't always existed and impacted communities of color. Rather, it was simply comfortable for White people to ignore or invalidate the caustic day-to-day reality people of color experience. Focusing on race and racism creates more visible internal conflict and discord; radical care demands this disruption.

CONDITIONS FOR ADOPTING AN ANTIRACIST STANCE

School leaders who adopt an antiracist stance understand how race features centrally in all aspects of life and especially within the institutions of school. We need only look at the 1954 *Brown v. Board of Education* decision for a reminder of the lengths that school systems go to in order to sidestep mandates to dismantle racist structures, including redrawing district lines and creating magnet or gifted programs that ultimately keep schools segregated (Bell, 1992; Delgado & Stefancic, 2017). Derrick Bell (1992) and other legal scholars who advanced critical race theory (CRT) recognized that the significant legal victories that had marked the previous 2 decades, particularly around school desegregation, were not having the intended impact of rolling back centuries of racism in the United States. Leaders who adopt an antiracist stance understand that racism is deeply embedded into the very fabric of our history and our institutions, and understand that their leadership practices have to reflect certain understandings.

Antiracist leaders understand several key truths. First, they recognize that racism is not aberrant; rather it is pervasive in all aspects of life and institutions. As such, they are particularly attuned to understanding how racism is functioning within the school, as well as in the historical, policy, and social contexts that impact the school system. As part of adopting an antiracist stance, leaders also embrace another CRT tenet of seeking out a wealth of counterstories that provide an alternative to dominant (i.e., White) narratives that have historically served to maintain persistent racial inequality. Besides providing a counternarrative, leaders who create spaces for storytelling are giving voice to historically marginalized people whose own experiences with oppression are often absent from representations of "truth." Second, hearing the stories can be a powerful tool that can disrupt the dysconcious racism—the distorted understandings about race and inequity (King, 1991)—that is prevalent in society by providing alternate perspectives and experiences to counter the construction of one version of reality (Ladson-Billings & Tate, 1995). Antiracist leadership, then, involves seeking out the counternarratives of Black and Latinx students, community, and staff members to better understand how to transform schools into more racially just spaces.

Third, antiracist leaders recognize how maintaining racism is both materially and socially beneficial to Whites (Delgado & Stefancic, 2017; Harris, 1993). That is to say that, for Whites, there is real value in maintaining racist structures. One need only look to redlining in housing to see how Whites can accumulate intergenerational wealth as a result of racist housing practices (Rothstein, 2017). Given the tangible and karmic benefits that Whites receive from racism, whether they seek out that benefit or not, it is not surprising that dismantling racist structures is *dis*incentivized. However, from time to time, when Whites champion the disruption of racist policies, it is typically because doing so benefits Whites; there is a convergence of interests. Even then, their action usually comes after a great deal of effort on the part of marginalized groups. Bell's argument, as it related to interest convergence, was that cases like *Brown v. Board of Education* had little to do with moral outrage about segregation and more to do with self-interests of elite Whites who were concerned with the international image and reputation of the United States. A more recent example of this can be found in the rise of the standardized testing "opt out" movement, which is largely dominated by middle-class Whites. While high-stakes testing has long been criticized within communities of color because of the impact of testing policies on curriculum, White parents were activated to resist the tests only after those impacts were felt within their children's schools (Rivera-McCutchen, 2021).

Finally, antiracist leaders understand that while race is socially constructed and not a biological determinant, it serves the purpose of advancing a false narrative of a genetically determined racial hierarchy that reinforces notions of White superiority over all other races. Though this is a critical understanding, antiracist leaders also acknowledge that the social construct of race in no way diminishes the very real and concrete ways that the construct has been legitimized and transformed into power and privilege in both material and social frames. Noted CRT legal scholar Cheryl Harris (1993) points out that

> Whites have come to expect and rely on these benefits, and over time these expectations have been affirmed, legitimated, and protected by the law. Even though the law is neither uniform nor explicit in all instances, in protecting settled expectations based on White privilege, American law has recognized a property interest in Whiteness that, although unacknowledged, now forms the background against which legal disputes are framed, argued, and adjudicated. (p. 1713)

"Whiteness" has afforded Whites, wittingly or not, with the privilege of shaping the way everyday life unfolds in ways that further the status and position of White people, especially in schools. Racial disparities in terms of access to educational opportunities illustrate how this plays out in schools on a consistent basis.

Given how deeply ingrained racism is throughout our society, conversations about schools must start with the premise that institutionalized and systematic racism are woven into the fabric of educational policy and, by extension, in the responses to policy (Ladson-Billings & Tate, 1995). Educational policy is often driven by the needs and interests of White students and their families. As López (2003) reminds us, "many times, we miss opportunities to identify and name racism, largely because we do not see it in the work we do and/or because our respective lenses are not attuned to recognizing it in our daily lives" (p. 86).

Leaders who embody an ethic of radical care are particularly attuned to racism, in the tradition of CRT, forming a foundation on which the other components of radical care are based. Through antiracist practices, leaders can thoughtfully engage in cultivating authentic relationships with members of the community, seeking to understand the impact that structural oppression has had on the students and families the school serves. School leaders who have adopted an antiracist stance also understand how educators' racial ideologies can lead to lowered expectations for their Black and Latinx students. In practicing radical care, leaders directly confront and disrupt racist ideologies and demand excellence of students and teachers, leveraging their power strategically to enact antiracist policy and practices. Finally, leaders' antiracist practices are firmly grounded in a spirit of radical hope for a future that is possible for Black and Latinx students.

WHEN ANTIRACIST PRACTICES ARE ABSENT

In the school highlighted in the chapter's opening vignette, a White principal failed to consistently engage the community around issues of race, and when he did engage, it was with a great deal of trepidation and discomfort. As a result of the leader's enactment of limiting care, many of the students and families likely experienced daily racial microaggressions, which scholars have defined as seemingly benign daily insults, either verbal or nonverbal, that reinforce systemic racial oppression (Solórzano & Pérez Huber, 2020). Further, these microaggressions create a hostile work environment for teachers of color who work to advocate on behalf of students and families (Kohli, 2018).

Often, leaders avoid talking about race and racism, and invoke the term *social justice* as a proxy for antiracism. This is a form of limiting care in that it avoids confronting race by placing an emphasis instead on social justice, a term generally concerned with advocating for equal rights for all, regardless of class, race, ethnicity, religion, gender, sexual identity, or any other historically marginalized group. While the specific definitions of social justice may vary, individuals, groups, or organizations typically use the term as a way to describe a particular kind of activism and advocacy in which they engage, and it takes shape in ways that are relevant for them. Using social justice as a substitute for antiracism is a manifestation of limiting care in that the focus is on a generalized set of conditions that students and families are experiencing, rather than on specific needs related to systemic racialized oppression. I argue, however, that a critical component of leading with radical care is an unwavering and explicit focus on antiracism itself, whereas social justice has the potential to allow people to escape an unrelenting focus on race and racism. By centering race and racism, leaders can leverage their authority to engage members of the school community in examining their own internalized racialized oppression and/or superiority, and to examine the impact and legacy of institutional racism.

Leaders who engage unapologetically in antiracist practices, rejecting the temptation to focus on social justice in place of racism, are able to fully confront racism within and outside of their institutions without equivocation. Unlike leaders practicing limiting care who are incapable of addressing the racial realities of schooling, either because they lack the moral courage or because they do not see it, leaders practicing radical care understand that engagement with race is nonnegotiable. They are able to engage in processes with their staff to either prevent racist incidents or directly confront racist practices. They engage others to encourage participation in a deeper process toward understanding how institutions, such as schools, are part of a broader framework of structural racism.

ADOPTING AN ANTIRACIST STANCE IN PRACTICE

As a Black man, Byron Johnson, the founding principal of the School for Social Justice middle school (SFSJ), saw himself in his students, and he was acutely aware of how structural racism impacted him and the community SFSJ serves. In my conversations with Johnson over the years and in his talks with his staff that I observed, he frequently and passionately cited the disparity in resource distribution between schools like SFSJ when compared to private, mostly White schools as a byproduct of structural racism. He argued that schools in more privileged and White communities organize student learning in ways that encouraged choice and exploration, while low-income schools in communities of color place an extraordinary emphasis on standardization and testing.

Johnson's commitment to antiracism was also evident in actions he took soon after several unarmed men were killed by police officers. Seeing both himself and his students in the deaths of Eric Garner, Alton Sterling, Philando Castile, Michael Brown, and Trayvon Martin, Johnson organized a rally, mobilizing students and staff who wanted to participate in a walkout to do so. Johnson's actions here represented an opportunity to publicly and forcefully speak out about racial oppression and policing. The rally gave voice not only to Johnson as a Black man, but also to the students, educators, and families of color who are impacted by structural oppression within policing.

Not stopping with the rally, Johnson searched for ways to use the deaths of Black men at the hands of police to catalyze structural changes in education and reached out to a broad network of school leaders and began conversations about organizing a full-day professional development conference around issues of race and racism in schooling. In December 2015, after a grand jury failed to indict the police officer who killed Eric Garner in Staten Island, Johnson emailed a message to a number of New York City (NYC) school leaders and educators outlining a 7-point plan of action, and an invitation to begin meeting. The points of action included the following:

1. Ensure that all of our youth as soon as they turn 18 are registered to vote.
2. Analyze current politicians and corporations and determine who is righteous and for us, and who is against us.

3. Organize communities to demand a school curriculum rooted in the beauty of Black and Brown history and culture.
4. Provide parenting courses and in-home mental health supports to at-risk parents and families.
5. Build and strengthen nursery and day care services in the most needy communities to close the language and executive function gap.
6. Determine the short- and long-term needs of our communities— *Think Globally.*
7. Exercise our second amendment rights.

After convening several meetings with a few area school principals, Johnson organized the Bronx Education Conference, which was convened during a citywide mandated professional development day, with race as the central focus. Several area schools joined the SFSJ staff at this conference, which included a keynote by Dr. Bree Picower, who spoke very directly about issues of White supremacy and structural racism in schools. Workshops facilitated throughout the day for breakout groups were also grounded in antiracism, and all conference attendees were given black T-shirts with the words "Bronx Ed Conference" in white lettering across the front and "#BlackLivesMatter" across the back.

By centering race in this conference and enacting radical care, Johnson intentionally created spaces for educators to reflect on how their pedagogy disrupted or maintained racial oppression. Attendees also had the opportunity to learn explicit strategies for revising their practices to align with antiracism. Far from being an isolated event, the Bronx Education Conference was part of ongoing efforts at SFSJ, but also represented a starting point for colleagues from other schools who attended to begin adopting antiracist practices. Much like the national Black Lives Matter at School movement, which started nearly a year later (Hagopian & Jones, 2020), the Bronx Education Conference was part of a larger effort to dismantle systemic oppression through radical care.

Johnson's actions—both the walkout and the organization of a conference explicitly focused on racism—were acts of radical care and stood in stark contrast to the overwhelming majority of school leaders across New York City, who did not take a public or proactive stand. Johnson's actions represent an enactment of radical care because he directly and unapologetically identified how institutional racism in policing was directly causing the death of Black men across the country. In so doing, Johnson demonstrated to his students and staff the need to confront issues of racism directly. Further, by engaging educators in antiracist practices Johnson sent a clear message to his Black and Latinx students that affirmed their worth and conveyed that their liberation and humanity was essential. Johnson's actions also contributed to the formation of authentic relationships, the second component of radical care, which I discuss in the next chapter.

Discussions about racism and social justice were already prominent at SFSJ prior to the education conference. In addition to Johnson ensuring that race and racism were integrated into the curriculum, they frequently covered them in the weekly Friday morning Community Circles, attended by all students, teachers, and staff. Further, Johnson initiated a partnership with Hip Hop Saves Lives, a nonprofit organization, in which students developed hip hop music videos posted on YouTube to address police brutality, economic and food justice, among other topics explicitly connected to racial inequality and their communities. One video, for example, features students going through their daily routines with their hands up to emphasize the normalization of the threat they faced as people of color from police officers, while rapping the lines "we will not be silent, we are unarmed civilians, no need for the violence" (Hip Hop Saves Lives, 2014). In other scenes, the students are seen marching through the streets with signs that say "Power to the People" and "End Racism," among other phrases. Johnson ensured that these videos were publicized on the school's website and used them as conversation starters at the weekly Community Circles.

As the examples above demonstrate, Johnson worked to engage in antiracist practices, the first component of radical care, very explicitly within his school, and worked to engage educators outside of his school, as well. His clarity on the existence and nature of racism facilitated his ability to enthusiastically and unrelentingly focus on race as a central feature of his work with his staff, students, and broader community. While the Bronx Education Conference was a major expression of Johnson's commitment to antiracist leadership, his daily work engaging his students and staff in critical discussions about the impact of structural racism also provide equally powerful examples of daily antiracist leadership practices. Critical examinations of race and racism permeated the SFSJ school. Johnson ensured that SFSJ teachers developed antiracist curricular materials that honored and affirmed Black and Latinx people and other people of color. This was evident in the literature they read by Black and Latinx authors, and in the emphasis on the history of Blacks that addressed more than slavery and struggle. Finally, Johnson's support for and encouragement of the students' videos that addressed racist police practices serve as evidence that when practicing radical care, there should be no daylight between conversations about racism and the actual work of schooling.

   Leaders who do not engage in antiracist practices, like Johnson does, either because they lack the moral courage or because they simply do not understand the impact of racism, foster a toxic culture where racial micro-aggressions, subtle everyday verbal and nonverbal racism, or even major racial incidents are the norm. They are enacting a form of limiting care and, as a result, structural racism and the systemic oppression of people of color is reproduced in covert and overt ways.

CONCLUSION

Radical care in leadership calls for explicit antiracism in daily practice. As Gooden reminds us, "leaders move beyond being good to actually doing good" (2020, para. 7). School leaders must engage their school communities in sustained conversations and processes that allow them to reflect on how they have internalized racism and examine how systemic oppression and structural racism are manifested in the school and other institutions. While rallies and conferences are major expressions of anti-racist practices, the day-to-day antiracist work must also be undertaken. For example, school leaders can engage their school community in equity audits to critically examine and revise their curricula, discipline practices, and teacher assignments so that they are more aligned with antiracist practices (Radd et al., 2021; Skrla et al., 2009). Leaders practicing radical care work unapologetically to create a culture within their school that is committed to antiracism in all aspects of their work. Finally, leaders who enact radical care also engage in the important work of understanding the racial history of the community and, in so doing, begin cultivating authentic relationships with families and community members.

CHAPTER 2

Component 2
Cultivating Authentic Relationships

One afternoon a number of years ago, I sat observing a small group of high school teachers meeting to discuss the progress of students who were in a program called "At Promise." The name of the program was intended to turn the notion of students being "at risk" on its head, but did, in fact, target students who were struggling. During the meeting, the teachers discussed various students' progress, and they turned their attention to John, who was late to school nearly every morning. One of the teachers shared that he was in temporary housing and was living in the Bronx with his family. This detail was critical because the school where the meeting was being held is in Staten Island, which is roughly 30 miles south of the Bronx. To get to school each morning, John had to commute for over 2 hours on multiple trains and take either a bus or ferry to reach the island. The teachers wondered why he didn't just transfer schools. They briefly discussed changing his schedule to accommodate his late arrival. They expressed sadness and some frustration, and then they moved on to discussing the next student.

The second component of radical care leadership is cultivating authentic relationships, and the vignette above is useful in highlighting the complex nature of this component. In the vignette, the teachers are trying to address John's frequent late arrival to school because of their concerns about the work he is missing. John's family had been living in Staten Island up until they became homeless, when they were moved into the only temporary housing space available to them, in the Bronx. The teachers' surprise about John revealed that, in fact, none of them seemed to know him very well. Losing one's home and moving into temporary housing is a protracted process, and yet this development in John's story was new to all but one of the teachers.

Certainly, John's circumstances were tragic, but the teachers in this meeting did not have the tools they needed to move beyond expressing their frustration or providing temporary and superficial relief for John.

In this situation, there was no attempt to better understand John's circumstances, nor to intervene in some way beyond addressing the immediate concern of him arriving to school on time. They failed to consider that the school was perhaps one of the most stable parts of his life and remaining in school was essential to his well-being. Rather, the teachers were practicing limiting care, focusing on the transactional experience of schooling, attending specifically to how John was expected to arrive and perform in school. Even if the choices and solutions to complex problems are not evident, as with John's circumstances, in schools where leaders prioritize the cultivation of authentic relationships, the conversation about John would have started long before his family was relocated to the Bronx. It would have gone beyond a schedule adjustment; it would have involved developing a plan for following up with John and his family and identifying needs and brainstorming solutions that placed value on John as a whole person, not just timely arrival to school. Further, these teachers' work would have been grounded in an understanding about the institutional oppression that led to the circumstances in the first place.

When leaders practice radical care, they create an expectation for their staff that every student is known well, and they create the structures within the school to ensure that authentic relationships are cultivated. The school leader would foster a climate within the school where educators understand that part of their role is to support family's needs beyond the academic demands. The vignette represents a failure of the school's principal to lead with radical care, which includes fostering a school climate through the establishment of norms and structures that place critical value on cultivating authentic relationships with the student.

CHARACTERISTICS OF AUTHENTIC RELATIONSHIPS

Unlike the relationships I describe above, leaders who practice radical care prioritize cultivating *authentic* relationships, which are marked by three characteristics: (1) love, (2) trust, and (3) an investment in the success of others. The first characteristic, love, is selfless and, resembling a familial quality, is borne out of a desire to protect and to provide for others, giving them more than even what we have (Jackson et al., 2014). It is a willingness to shield others from pain and to right injustices. The second characteristic of authentic relationships is trust, which makes way for honesty and the ability to make mistakes without risk of loss. Finally, investment in the success of others begins with a profound interest in others' well-being and a desire to connect personally with all who cross their paths. Leaders who practice radical care cultivate relationships that transcend transactions. They understand that doing so will lead to the other person's success.

When school leaders and other educators have authentic relationships with their students, families, and community members, they do a better job of identifying interests and gaps that might exist in services and programs. There is a myriad of ways that leaders can facilitate opportunities to build deep and authentic relationships with the family and community members, expanding the role of the school beyond its walls, even if the educators don't live within the same community. Engaging in neighborhood walks (University Council for Educational Administration., n.d.) and conducting community equity audits (Green, 2016), for example, are activities explicitly designed to disrupt deficit narratives about communities. These practices help educators see the students' and families' inherent community cultural wealth (Yosso, 2005), as well as understand how challenges facing communities are typically the result of systemic and structural oppression, rather than inherent to the people who live in those communities. Moreover, these practices can catalyze partnerships with community members, bridging the social capital of educators with that of the community to work toward transformation (Ishimaru, 2020; Warren & Mapp, 2011; Watson, 2020).

Being attuned to the broader community helps leaders foster culture inside the school wherein authentic relationships are part of the norms of the daily work between and among the educators and the children they teach (Curry, 2016). School leaders practicing radical care work understand the importance of cultivating authentic relationships with their teachers because it creates opportunities for educators to feel trusted and supported to innovate and refine their practice. Leaders who cultivate authentic relationships with their staff model the kinds of connections teachers need to develop with their students, which are also grounded in trust and support. All of these relationships within the school also create a foundation for an expectation of excellence, which I discuss further in the next chapter. Since the relationships are not transactional, or focused on performance for performance's sake, expecting excellence is borne out of an authentic desire to see someone who is cared for be successful.

In schools where leaders practice radical care and place value in the cultivation of authentic relationships, the leaders don't see themselves at the top of a hierarchical structure. Rather, in many ways, they see themselves as equal to their staff, as well as their students and families and caregivers they serve. In a formal sense, there is a hierarchical dynamic, but the structure feels "flatter" because people at all levels of structure are brought into the processes of decisionmaking, and there is a conscious effort to create a more equal distribution of power. With the power more evenly distributed, relationships based on trust can be developed, free of concern over misuse of power or vulnerability. Leaders who practice radical care understand that building deeply authentic relationships with students is crucial to building trust, an essential quality that allows for learners to take risks, fail, then learn from those failures. Similarly, authentic relationships between the leaders and teachers also create opportunities for the adults to innovate, take risks, fail, and learn.

Along with encouraging risk-taking, authentic relationships require honesty about failure and opportunities for improvement. If there is a mutual trust, then honesty can exist. Adults and students can be honest about their disappointment, or if they expect something better. And the person on the receiving end of the authentic care is also able to try new things and take risks because they know that the care is unconditional, even when they fail. They are encouraged to take risks, and they are encouraged to do better because they know that they are cared for and they don't want to disappoint others. More importantly, they get to a point where they don't want to let themselves down, because the care that has been demonstrated toward them has helped to develop deeper relationships with themselves.

CONDITIONS FOR CULTIVATING AUTHENTIC RELATIONSHIPS

Under the framework of radical care, urban school leaders see the strengths and assets of the communities they serve. Unlike those that practice limiting care, leaders practicing radical care ascribe to Yosso's (2005) theory of "community cultural wealth," which acknowledges and values the cultural capital that is inherent in communities of color. Rather than valuing wealth and income, leaders who are engaged in cultivating authentic relationships within their communities value other forms of capital that are typically ignored or devalued, including linguistic, navigational, social, and resistant capital, among others described by Yosso. There is a wealth of expertise and knowledge within the communities urban schools serve, and leaders practicing radical care embrace opportunities to build relationships that can lead to equitable collaborations with communities (Ishimaru, 2020).

Cultivating authentic relationships is critical to understanding historical institutional trauma that is often part of the DNA of schools and the communities they serve, particularly in underserved communities

(Horsford, 2011). There are layers upon layers of historical pain that need to be understood and unpacked because, in many underserved communities, there is a deep-seated distrust of institutions that comes from intergenerational experiences of being targeted and maligned. Authentic relationships, then, must involve leaders exploring important questions, including: How does this trauma manifest with respect to how families view the institution of schooling? How might this history act as a barrier to accessing all that schools might offer? How is this distrust and skepticism manifested in the relationships between the schools and the families?

Enrique Alemán offers a powerful example of why understanding community history is a crucial part of cultivating authentic relationships in his documentary, *Stolen Education* (Luna, 2013). The film explores the experiences of Mexican American families in Driscoll, Texas, who challenged the legality of a policy where children with Spanish surnames, including Alemán's mother, were forced to repeat the 1st grade for several years. Like countless other examples of "creative noncompliance" in violation of desegregation laws, this district policy had the effect of stifling the academic progress of an entire generation of individuals. In school, Alemán's mother learned that being Latinx and speaking Spanish were not considered assets; rather, they were liabilities that incurred discriminatory treatment. This linguistic terrorism had a long-lasting impact on entire generations of Latinx youth like Alemán's who were explicitly not taught Spanish as a way to protect them from potential harm in school, the very institution that supposedly aimed to help educate them (Anzaldúa, 2012; Martínez & Rivera-McCutchen, forthcoming). Cultivating authentic relationships with community members allows school leaders to learn about the communities' history and results in a deeper understanding of how oppression has impacted them, often across generations.

These examples underscore what one Bronx middle school principal shared with me: very often, the parents and caregivers whose children attend the neighborhood schools have themselves not had positive interactions with institutions in general, and schools specifically. Frequently, parents may have attended the very same school and may have had traumatizing experiences there when they were children. They may have been targeted by an excessively punitive system, labeled as challenged, denied opportunities for acceleration, or been victimized by their teachers' low expectations and doubts of their worth. Beyond this, parents and caregivers of children currently attending schools may have witnessed their own parents being devalued within the school when they were children. As a result, there is a skepticism and fear involved in interacting with the school agency. Leaders must prioritize cultivating authentic relationships as a way to confront the history, through love, trust, protection, and an investment in the success of the communities they serve.

School leaders practicing radical care have to be intentional about creating a community wherein authentic relationships are a foundational practice. Here, it's important to again underscore the interlocking nature of the components of radical care. Cultivating authentic relationships can only happen if the leader has adopted an antiracist stance and understands institutional oppression. They recognize that authentic relationships lead to a deeper investment in everyone's success and capacity to excel. These relationships must be grounded in a deep understanding of community history and are informed by an acute awareness of racism, the politics of power, and their impact on the schooling of children who have historically been oppressed. They are keenly aware of the dynamics of power, and they are strategic about how they leverage their authority to challenge oppressive practices and structures within and outside of the school community. Finally, these relationships hold leaders accountable and propel them forward to embrace radical hope, an unwavering belief that transformation is possible. Leaders who cultivate authentic relationships earn the trust of students, families, and the broader community, moving beyond performative and superficial relationships.

WHEN AUTHENTIC RELATIONSHIPS ARE ABSENT

Relationships in schools are complex because of the power dynamics that exist among the various groups and individuals and can serve as a barrier to cultivating authentic relationships. Consider that school leaders have positional authority over pedagogical and nonpedagogical staff, as well as students and families within their school communities. Teachers also have power over their students, and by extension, students' families. These power dynamics can inhibit the development of authentic relationships because the hierarchical nature of the relationships can limit the development of trust. As a result, a more transactional relationship emerges where there is no love, no trust, and no investment in the success of other. When relationships exist solely at the transactional level, barriers are created and the students and adults in the school cannot feel that they can safely take risks. In these environments, teachers are not willing to try innovative practices, and students are fearful of participating in class unless they are certain they have the "right" response. What results is limiting care, because the emphasis is on how everyone performs in school rather than on building trust and transforming schools into a place where risk-taking and learning from failure are key features.

When leaders fail to foster a culture where cultivating authentic relationships is a central part of the school, the deep investment in the success of others, a characteristic of authentic relationships, is also lacking. An essential part of cultivating authentic relationships involves getting to know the needs and desires of the community to better support the students they teach. In the case of John, the student in the opening vignette, his teachers did not look at the structural oppression that undergirded his late arrival, and as a result were limited in their abilities to consider how to fundamentally transform the opportunities he would have. Since the relationship is focused on the transaction of schooling solely, the attention shifts from understanding the needs of the whole child to ensure long-term success to what is happening in the moment, during the hours of school. Educators who have authentic relationships focus on the structural challenges rather than the symptoms manifested by a particular behavior or practice. This focus on the symptom rather than the root of oppression often has implications in how schools operate, with attention paid to "feel good" initiatives that are fundamentally incompatible with the needs, desires, or interests of the community.

When authentic relationships are absent, educators are also not deeply invested in the success of their peers. They are practicing limiting care with each other. Their relationships are superficial and performative with little attention paid to how each educator can support one another to constantly refine and improve their pedagogical practices. Standards for teaching and learning are lowered and this has profoundly negative consequences for the students and the teachers. While lowering expectations in the moment may be easy and feel like an accomplishment, in the long-term, they limit the possibilities for everyone's success.

CULTIVATING AUTHENTIC RELATIONSHIPS IN PRACTICE

The value of authentic relationships in schools is not a new phenomenon; in fact, historical antecedents can provide insight into what this looks like in action. For guidance, we can look back to the tradition of Black educators, particularly the principalship in segregated schools in the South. Although there has been greater attention paid to the promise of such schools in more recent years, thanks to scholars such as Vanessa Siddle Walker (1996), Lenoar Foster and Linda Tillman (2009),

Sonya Douglass Horsford (2010, 2011), and others, many are still far too limited in their understanding of these schools, in large part due to a false narrative that all segregated Black schools were inferior. While these schools were certainly starved of resources in comparison to their White counterparts, what they lacked in material wealth, they often more than made up for in the depth of the authentic relationships and how those relationships leveraged a depth of rigor in teaching (Siddle Walker, 1996; Siddle Walker & Archung, 2003). Principals and faculty lived, shopped, and prayed alongside their students and were part of the broader community. Moreover, Black educators saw themselves as stewards, creating better opportunities for the children and the families they served. These close daily relations were a foundation that led to authentic relationships between educators and students.

Despite the significant changes in a post-*Brown* era, there are examples of contemporary leaders and schools who have worked to cultivate authentic relationships reminiscent of those found in segregated Black schools. For example, Bridges Institute is a high school located in a Bronx community that has been historically oppressed and is chronically underresourced. Students entering the high school have generally been denied access to high-quality educational experiences. The school was designed to cultivate authentic relationships that could then be leveraged to support students' academic success. Let's compare the leadership reaction at Bridges to the vignette above.

Mike, an alum of Bridges High School, recalled that in his final year he struggled to get to school on time. The principal, Mary Norwood, arranged for the school's parent coordinator to call him daily. He recalled that she called every single morning at around 7 a.m., staying on the phone until Mike got up. Then 10 minutes later, she would call back again, asking: "Mike, you up? You in the shower?" It was not enough to put the responsibility fully on Mike for his own success. At Bridges, the leader created a culture where everyone in the school wanted him to succeed and shared that responsibility. As Mike recalled, they made sure kids got to school. The kind of attention that Mike received was grounded in a desire to ensure the success of the students, doing whatever it took. That is to say, this leader understood that the student must be physically in the school in order to be part of a learning community that was dedicated to progress and liberation; in order for that to happen, the student had to be called each day to ensure that he would be present.

The interaction with Mike was not an isolated incident. Another alum, Henry, shared that every night his parents were gone from home because they had to work in order to support the family. Even then, the family just got by. This left him and his two brothers to their own devices, with just enough food. As Henry recalled, he and his brothers had to raise themselves in a tough neighborhood. As a result, his guard was typically up. However, the school represented a safe haven where authentic familial and caring relationships were always present. Beyond physical safety, Henry knew he was safe psychologically and emotionally. He recalled the principal and teachers facilitating trust-building activities that were intentionally designed to build community.

The authentic relationships are not about just getting students through classes. They become bridges so that students can return to the community and share their success. One student in particular, Lydia, required a great deal of nurturing and involvement from all of her teachers, and her then-advisor, Mary Norwood. Lydia described her home life as challenging, and she struggled to make it to school. Lydia was supported throughout school and successfully graduated from Bridges. She went on to college where she still found herself struggling at times. However, because of the authentic relationship Mary had developed with her, Lydia knew she could reach out to Mary for support; Lydia was able to successfully earn her college degree. She later became a paraprofessional at Bridges, where she was hired by Mary, who had become the principal. Though she struggled to pass the teacher certification exams, she was ultimately successful and later became a teacher at Bridges. Mary encouraged her to pursue a leadership degree and certification, and after some time, Lydia did; she is now the assistant principal at Bridges, the same high school where she was nurtured and supported.

Stories describing the kinds of authentic relationships similar to the one Mary and Lydia shared as teacher and student are prevalent among Bridges alum. In an interview with one graduate of the school, Andres shared the following reflection:

> It wasn't like we weren't just like a bunch of stupid kids. At first, with Mary, I felt like, I mean that she really cared about you, you know, to me she [was] like my at-school mom whereby she wanted to understand, she wanted me to get it, she wanted me to grow. I don't think I had that throughout my years at a lot of schools. . . . My guess is that I'm better for going to Bridges. Looking back at what I experienced and I think a lot of it has to do with the staff, because you know, I felt like they did really connect with us and they had a vested interest, and making sure that we succeeded, and that we were participating, and that we actually cared.

In reflecting on his experience years after leaving Bridges, Andres described authentic relationships between the staff members and the students. The adults in the school, even the "lunch lady," as he described her, wanted to connect with the students. Andres understood those relationships as being part of a desire that he and his peers could succeed and could be invested in their own success. These relationships were grounded in love, trust, and an investment in the students' success. In the instance when students are failing, a leader who practices radical care leverages the authentic relationships to better understand the causes of the failure.

Another contemporary example of where authentic relationships are being fostered is at the School for Social Justice. During the Martin Luther King Jr. National Day of Service one year, Byron Johnson, a Bronx middle school principal, partnered with the Black Googlers Network, a group of Black Google employees providing service to communities of color, to open the school's doors to provide learning and recreational opportunities for families and community members. In addition to providing workshops on coding and computers for kids, Johnson and his school staff also set up stations in the gym for community attendees to learn about the Black experience in America, from slavery to present. The event was staffed by volunteers drawn from the community as well as the school teaching and pedagogical staff. During this event, Johnson capitalized on the school being centrally located to create an opportunity to bring families and community members together. Not only did community members attend, but the school's teachers and their families were interacting with each other, cultivating authentic relationships with one another.

Another year, during a Black Lives Matter in Schools event, Johnson used his school's central location in the neighborhood to create a hub of activism and resources for community members. Drawing from his deep knowledge of the needs and assets within the community, the event was designed to provide opportunities for all community members and nonprofit organizations to bridge social capital. Parents and kids and others from the community selected workshops to attend, with topics including tenant advocacy, voter registration, school integration, and other timely topics. By focusing the event on advocacy issues relevant to the community, Johnson and the school staff were able to deepen the relationships with community members.

A powerful way for school leaders and their staff to build authentic relationships where the community is known deeply is to engage in events in the neighborhood. Festivals, block parties, and community events sponsored by local organizations, including churches and other faith-based organizations, provide school members the opportunities to see their students and families outside of the school context. This goes a long way toward humanizing everyone; however, it is all too uncommon. Teachers come and go with blinders on, completely oblivious of the community that surrounds the school. School leaders should also attend community events with families and create a culture where their staff do the same.

In New York City, the Community Schools initiative was implemented to formalize a community-minded approach to education. To that end, schools formally designated as Community Schools received local, state, and federal funding to integrate a number of programs to provide wrap-around services to kids, families, and the residents in the neighborhood. The goal was to "transform the school building into a natural hub of local activity, vitality, culture, support, and education for the broader community" (NYC Department of Education, 2015, p. 15). These kinds of initiatives do a good job of building a hub of resources in the school and integrating needed services that benefit students and other members of the families. This might include medical, dental, and vision care, as well as mental health services. Fundamentally, when families' essential and basic needs are met, schools can truly address the academic work, so schools are a logical location for these services. Although some schools have a formal designation as a "Community School" with a menu of resources offered to neighborhood residents, not having a formal designation should not preclude a school from building deep authentic relationships with students and their families. School leaders who practice radical care find creative ways to connect and partner with community organizations. If schools can be places that provide critical assistance, we can begin healing historic institutional trauma and build authentic relationships.

In some cases, schools adopt an advisory model to carve out a nonacademic space for students to connect with one another and an adult at the school. Unlike a homeroom, where all sorts of administrative and transactional activities happen—attendance is taken, forms and information are distributed, coats are put away—advisory is predicated on the belief that students need a space to explore topics ranging from interpersonal challenges to college and/or career choices. It is a place where authentic relationships can be developed and students can be known as whole people, outside of their academic identities. This is particularly important as kids get older and schools begin to departmentalize, and the student to teacher ratio increases substantially. In my first year as a teacher at a small Bronx high school, I was assigned an advisory of 9th-graders. These 20 students were also in my Humanities class. We spent that first year getting to know one another, and their remaining years in high school deepening our relationship. While there was some attrition and some new additions, the cohesiveness of our advisory was unwavering.

As a result of the relationships I developed with students in the advisory class, I forged deeper connections with them and their families beyond the formal advisory structure. When one student was diagnosed with cancer and had to be homeschooled (she later fully recovered), I visited her and her family frequently. When another did not have plans for the prom, I went home, found a dress that might fit her, and picked her up to take her with me. Her mother, who was highly protective, was at ease with me taking her. At my advisory students' graduation, I cried like a baby, bursting with pride, and I hugged them and their families tightly. When I got married a few years later, my husband and I intentionally found a central location that was easily accessible by train so that they could attend the wedding ceremony. When one student later graduated from college 6 hours away from New York City, I drove up to attend because the travel was not feasible for his family members. And when it became clear that transitioning back to the city might be challenging, I made sure he had the resources he needed to return. When I had my first child, a number of them came to my home in the Bronx to visit my newborn. In the years since, I have held their babies, attended weddings and funerals, and continued to visit them. I developed authentic relationships with their families and, as a result, family members knew that they could entrust their beloved children to me.[1]

Unlike the advisory model that was implemented at the Bronx high school where I taught, some school leaders assign advisories to all adult staff members in the school, including nonpedagogical staff, leaning heavily on the proverb "it takes a village" to raise healthy children. Moreover, expanding advisories to include other nonpedagogical adults in the school humanizes the institution as a whole, especially for the parents and family members whose own experiences as children in schools may have been traumatic. It also increases the opportunities for the school to connect with families and caregivers, forming deeply authentic relationships. By decreasing the adult-to-student ratio, the responsibility of building connections with students and families becomes part of the fabric of schooling. Advisors can connect with caregivers and family members when challenges need to be addressed, but also when successes need to be celebrated. It is important to note that the authentic relationships established in advisories are not intended to supplant high academic standards and achievement. Rather, cultivating authentic relationships meets the fundamental socioemotional needs of students. Once those needs are met, leaders practicing radical care encourage educators to leverage the relationships to push for greater academic outcomes.

Leaders practicing radical care can also work to develop authentic relationships through thoughtful organization of the instruction and assessment design that emphasizes process over product. For example, leaders in schools that belong to the New York Performance Consortium rejected high-stakes examinations typically used in high schools across the state because focusing on the tests reinforced transactional relationships and limiting care, rather than authentic relationships and radical care. Students in Consortium schools are tasked with completing portfolios or exhibitions of some type that demonstrate not only mastery of a subject and standard, but also the process by which the student arrived at the outcome (New York Performance Standards Consortium, n.d.). First developed as a handful of schools, the Consortium now includes nearly 40 high schools from across New York State, although most are concentrated in New York City. Focusing on alternative approaches to high-stakes evaluation requires a great deal of effort and collaboration, all in the interest of supporting students to be academically successful. This requires that staff build deeply connected relationships with their students and with each other.

While this is not always a perfect process, the premise is that helping students succeed academically requires understanding them as whole people, not just as students sitting in their classrooms. Students engage in projects that culminate in performance-based assessment tasks (PBATs) that typically require deep inquiry and an extended engagement and process (Hantzopoulos et al., 2021). Students then defend those PBATs to a group of teachers and volunteers from the community who evaluate the work with a common rubric. The interaction between the students and evaluators is deep and reveals an underlying authentic relationship. Frequently, students are required to revise their work and present again. When it works well, the moment, though tense, is profoundly moving because the conversation around the need for revisions is framed around expectations, but also by authentic relationships and radical care. Teachers communicate to students how they will be there to support the students as they take risks and work to achieve success. They are difficult conversations that, absent authentic relationships, would likely result in students being discouraged and unwilling to revise and try again. However, because they are grounded first in deep connections, students can recognize that the push to revisit their work is fundamentally coming from a place of radical care.

CONCLUSION

Cultivating authentic relationships begins when leaders work with staff members to develop a deep knowledge and respect for the community's history and experiences. Leaders must create the expectation that this is a part of belonging to the school's community when the hiring process begins. School leaders who practice radical care and work to cultivate authentic relationships know that personal connections are created, fostered, and developed first by knowing the community in which their schools are situated. They understand that the school is an extension of the community, and in order to know the kids who attend the school, they need to know the community. They have a sense of the community's history, as well as its challenges and assets. They know where their students live and what challenges they and their families may face, because it helps them understand what may be limiting the student, but also what can enable the student's success. In other words, they understand that the professional is deeply personal, and they work not only to build connections between themselves and others, but also to foster an environment where those connections between all of the adults and children in the school are deliberately created so that love, trust, and an investment in others' success is always present.

Orientations and teacher professional development should involve community walks and other dedicated opportunities to connect with stakeholders who can highlight the strengths of the neighborhood and help educators understand the challenges in the context of the community's history and systemic oppression. School leaders can also create opportunities within the school to foster authentic relationships. This requires thinking creatively about how to build structures within the school that maximize connections between the adults and students. Authentic relationships can then be leveraged to demand excellence from students and teachers.

CHAPTER 3

Component 3

Believing in Students' and Teachers' Capacity for Excellence

One afternoon, I sat observing a professional development meeting led by Mary Norwood, the principal, where a small group of Humanities teachers were discussing a sample of student writing. Most of the teachers had strong critiques of the student work including but not limited to a lack of a coherent thesis, insufficient evidence to support an argument, and lack of opposing viewpoints. Still, when Norwood asked the teachers to rate the paper using a common rubric, none of the teachers indicated that they would have asked the student to revise. Noting my surprise after the meeting, Ms. Norwood revealed that she believed teachers approached student work from a model of deficit thinking. She believed that these teachers lowered their standards for their students because they perceived that since the students had so many problems in their personal lives, what they were achieving was sufficient.

The exercise was intended to lead teachers through a process of norming a common writing rubric, using a piece of student work. The teachers were able to agree on the significant flaws in the student's work, and yet they also agreed that the student would receive a "competent" on the rubric without requiring any revisions. Despite the teachers very clearly identifying a number of strong critiques about student work, they seemed to be unwilling to indicate that the work had fallen below standard on the rubric. The teachers never uttered disparaging words about the students or about their academic abilities. However, by refusing to demand more from the students, they revealed an unspoken, yet deeply held belief about the limits of what they believed these students could achieve. In failing to expect more from the students, these teachers were practicing a form of limiting care. Although the principal here was able to explicitly identify how the teachers' conversation about students was grounded in deficit perspectives, she failed to push the teachers to examine or reflect on this; she, too, was practicing limiting care. Rather than pause the exercise and explicitly interrogate their decision and highlight the deficit perspectives about what students were capable of doing, the principal let it go.

This vignette highlights the complexity of leading with radical care, and challenges even the most committed leaders. While Norwood demonstrated the capacity to cultivate authentic relationships (see Chapter 2), in this example, she hesitated to directly engage the teachers in a difficult conversation about their perspectives. Consequently, Norwood all but assured that the students who were the focus of the teachers' conversation never received the support they needed to develop a coherent thesis, learn to use evidence, and integrate opposing viewpoints effectively to support and strengthen their own argument. However, a leader practicing radical care in this situation would have embraced it as an opportunity to directly highlight the misalignment between how the teachers talked about the work and the next steps they would take with the students. The principal might begin by asking teachers to articulate what would strengthen the students' papers and how they might teach those specific skills. Eliciting responses to these initial questions would allow the principal to then ask the teachers to discuss how they arrived at their decision to not require revision despite their strong critiques. In this kind of interaction, the principal would work to surface the teachers' deficit mindsets while encouraging them to reflect on their practices in general. Throughout this process, a leader practicing radical care demonstrates that they believe teachers have the capacity for growth and excellence, while also modeling how they want their teachers to hold this belief for their students. Leaders who practice radical care can leverage their authentic relationships with their teachers to engage them in challenging conversations about student capacity like this situation warranted.

The vignette above helps to highlight two critical points about believing in students' and teachers' capacity to be excellent, the third component of radical care. First, if leaders don't expect teachers to be excellent, through challenging their thinking and creating a culture of reflective practice, teachers might fail to demand it of themselves. Leaders who practice radical care make it clear to their teachers that they will challenge them to consider how their words and beliefs may translate into practices that limit the rigor and challenge in their pedagogy. If leaders fail to explicitly call out teacher practices and narratives that reflect deficit beliefs about their students, they are failing to practice a core component of radical care. Second, when leaders do not challenge teachers in these ways, the leaders do harm by failing to create an environment where educators believe students have the capacity to do challenging work, think critically, and engage in thoughtful problem solving, despite the difficulties students may face in their lives outside of school. Students' long-term success is limited when their teachers do not believe that they are capable of engaging in challenging academic work.

BELIEVING IN THE CAPACITY FOR EXCELLENCE

The third component of a radical care framework is believing in students' and teachers' capacity for excellence. Here I draw from the literature on deeper learning and define student excellence as having the ability and skills to think critically, work collaboratively, and engage in complex problem solving (Burns et al., 2019; Noguera et al., 2015). Likewise, excellence for teachers involves similar skills in service of supporting their students to achieve excellence. Belief in students' and teachers' capacity for excellence is marked by a few key characteristics: (1) seeing potential for growth, (2) explicitly articulating expectations for achieving excellence, (3) providing resources, and (4) modeling taking and learning from risks. While the characteristics are similar for what it means to believe in capacity for excellence in students as well as teachers, it is useful to tease them apart for the purpose of clarity and precision. Leaders and teachers alike need to believe in students' capacity for excellence. But leaders practicing radical care must also have this belief about teachers, or they risk adopting a deficit mindset about the capacity of teachers to be excellent, meeting and exceeding their potential.

Leaders practicing radical care fundamentally believe that all students have the potential for growth. As a result, they demand that students be held to high standards because there is a central belief in their ability to always do better. They believe that the students can succeed, provided that the barriers and limitations resulting from systemic oppression are eliminated. As Donna Harris, a grassroots activist and New Rochelle resident who was advocating on behalf of Black and Latinx students and other students of color in the district, said once, "Our children are geniuses! Treat them as such!" Harris's exclamation, echoes Asa Hilliard III's call decades earlier to "release the genius" (1991, p. 34) of Black children and underscores the importance of the mindset that is central for leaders practicing this component: Black and Latinx students are more than capable of engaging in academically challenging work. It is the job of the school to create the opportunities for them to demonstrate their inherent genius. This requires creating a culture where there is an expectation that students are capable of limitless potential. This is especially important when kids have entered schools significantly underprepared in prior school settings.

Leaders who practice radical care are also explicit with students that they expect excellence from them. Having high expectations is about challenging students, even if (perhaps, especially if) they are lacking academic skills we believe they should have already learned given their age and grade in school. School leaders must create an environment where all educators believe in their students' inherent greatness and their capacity to be even greater. This issue of capacity is a critical part of having high expectations because it's not necessarily about what the student can do at a given moment. Rather, it's an understanding and a belief that, but for a lack of opportunity or resources, students might be able to accomplish any challenge they may face (Irvine, 1991, 2003). So leaders who believe in students' capacity for excellence are also committed to providing appropriate resources, supports, and scaffolds to help students meet their full potential.

A final characteristic of this component is modeling for students what it looks like to push yourself, take risks, make mistakes, and learn from failure. School leaders who practice radical care must be clear that expecting excellence should not be confused with expecting perfection. Rather, achieving excellence is an ongoing effort to improve by capitalizing on experience and failure. School leaders have to be public learners and model this behavior for students to emulate.

The school leaders must also have high expectations for their teachers who work with students on a daily basis. The principal alone cannot have high expectations for students. As noted scholar Asa Hilliard III (1991) explained,

> Just as there is a vast untapped potential, yes, genius, among the children, there is also a vast untapped potential among the teachers who serve the children. I believe that the intellectual and professional potential of our teachers has been drastically underestimated, as a consequence of the same paradigm that causes us to underestimate the intellectual and professional potential of our students. (p. 36)

It is incumbent upon the leaders, then, to disrupt these limiting care paradigms and build teachers' capacity for excellence. Just as students must be viewed as being full of untapped potential, so too must teachers be viewed. Teachers have the capacity for growth, regardless of rhetoric that says otherwise. The truth is that most teachers really do want to deepen their practice. Leaders practicing radical care reject deficit mindsets about teachers and view each teacher as having the potential for growth and improvement. Radical care, then, demands that leaders expect greatness out of teachers and that they cultivate an environment where there are multiple opportunities for teachers to renew their enthusiasm and dedication to their professional learning.

Just as they must do with students, leaders practicing radical care must also clearly articulate to teachers that they expect excellence from them. Leaders need to be clear with teachers that they believe teachers have the potential to continuously hone and refine their practice. Just as with students, these expectations must be coupled with deep support for teachers. Leaders must provide resources, training, and feedback to support teachers' ongoing success. And just as instruction for students must be differentiated, leaders must provide differentiated supports to meet teachers where they are. This includes providing models of what excellent teaching looks like, including how teachers can best provide supports for students.

Finally, believing in teachers' capacity to be excellent requires that the leader models taking risks for the sake of improvement and learning from failure. The leader must be a public learner and show vulnerability around failure and trying again, making these efforts and reflections part of the narrative of what it means to work toward excellence in teacher practice.

CONDITIONS FOR PROMOTING EXCELLENCE

Like the other components of radical care, this third component, believing in the capacity for excellence, depends on the other parts of the radical care framework. Leaders whose practices are grounded in an ethic of radical care understand how institutional oppression contributes to the construction of low expectations, particularly for Black and Latinx children, and other racialized groups (Foster, 1998; Hilliard, 1991; Irvine, 2003; Liou et al., 2016; Valenzuela, 1999; Wilson, 2015). They understand that lowered expectations for students in the short-term can severely limit students' opportunities in the long-term. These leaders fundamentally believe that students are capable of meeting rigorous academic standards, provided that they have the appropriate supports from the school and their teachers. It means also that leaders must support teachers in developing their own deep understanding of how institutional oppression has impacted students' educational opportunities and outcomes. This is especially important when kids arrive at school significantly underprepared because they have been denied access to a high-quality and rigorous instruction in their prior school settings. Having high expectations is about challenging students, even if they are lacking skills that we believe they should have already learned. School leaders must create an environment where all educators believe in their students' inherent greatness and in their own capacity to be even greater.

Kids do not come to school from homes that are devoid of value or worth. Rather, they bring with them a rich and deep cultural knowledge, and a set of values that their families have taught them (Foster, 1998; Solórzano & Yosso, 2002; Yosso, 2005). Expecting academic excellence requires that school leaders work to build upon students' and families' knowledge (Antrop-González & De Jesús, 2006; Curry, 2016) and create experiences for students that will prepare them academically, regardless of their prior access to high-quality formalized education (Yamamura et al., 2010). It is about disabusing ourselves of the belief that simply because students have not yet been taught certain academic skills they are inherently not as capable as their peers who have.

Leaders who practice radical care must have explicit conversations around how racism can unconsciously impact how we think about what students are or are not capable of achieving, particularly those who have been marginalized. Antiracist practices, the first component of radical care, enable leaders to engage teachers in reflection around their curricular and instructional decisions, always asking, "Is this rigorous enough?" Where the answer is "no," teachers must ask themselves "why?" Practices that are lacking in rigor must be publicly surfaced and interrogated to better understand how curricula and instructional practices reproduce structural inequality (Picower, 2021). Leaders have to regularly create spaces for that kind of inner and public dialogue to happen.

To engage in this challenging work, therefore, leaders have to also ensure that the relationships in the schools are deeply authentic, the second component of radical care. Teachers and students must feel as though they are part of a community where they can safely take risks in their learning (Hantzopolous, 2016; Tyner-Mullings, 2012, 2015). Everyone in the school should feel secure about being honest in identifying how they're struggling and when they need support so that they can continue to work toward excellence. Authentic relationships help to create the conditions where a belief in excellence is possible.

Leveraging power, the fourth component of radical care, is one of the ways leaders work strategically to cultivate a school culture of belief in excellence. Believing that teachers and students can be successful is of little worth if we are unable to access the material resources that they need to reach their capacity and beyond. Leaders practicing radical care leverage their power to address the ways oppression is manifested inside their buildings, as well as in the policies that impact their school communities (Bass, 2012, 2016; Wilson, 2016). Leaders must clear the path and create the conditions that allow each person to fulfill their utmost potential.

Finally, radical hope, the fifth component of the framework, is what undergirds the belief in the capacity for excellence. For leaders who practice radical care, their belief about the capacity for excellence tends to begin long before they entered schools of education for their teacher or leadership training. In conversations about their beliefs, leaders rarely mentioned their teacher educator or leadership programs as the catalysts for developing these beliefs. Rather, they were grounded in their lives from an early age and came from a more personal connection. They have been taught through the actions of their communities and families that they are capable and powerful and that they can achieve anything they set their minds to. These are the individuals who should be identified to lead urban schools because they are already calibrated to believe in everyone's capacity to achieve more than they believe themselves capable of. ·

LIMITING CARE APPROACHES TO EXCELLENCE

In the following sections I describe two approaches that are often thought of as synonymous with achieving excellence. The first, which I describe as "bootstrap" frameworks, addresses grit and growth mindset theories, which center individual efforts as levers for success. The second addresses the use of high-stakes testing policies that aim to mandate excellence through accountability. While these two general approaches seem appealing, in fact, they are examples of limiting care.

"Bootstrap" Frameworks

At first glance, growth mindset (Dweck, 2006), grit (Duckworth, 2018), and other similar frameworks seem well-aligned with the notions of capacity for excellence I've been describing in this chapter. Dweck argues that individuals with a fixed mindset tend to be limited in their success because they believe that skills and ability are innate and cannot be cultivated, whereas those with a growth mindset are likely to thrive because believe they can develop their skills and talents through hard work and effort. Duckworth's theory of grit similarly suggests that passion, perseverance, and dedication over time, despite setbacks, are essential for individual success. Certainly, Black and Latinx communities have demonstrated an incredible amount of resiliency *despite* the systemic forces that are working against them (Goodman, 2018; Love, 2019).

The problem with "bootstrap" frameworks is that they locate the work and struggle within the individual teachers and students who must transform themselves in order to be successful. Yet, as Ladson-Billings (2006) powerfully described, the problem is structural and systemic given that the United States has amassed "historic, economic, sociopolitical, and moral debt" toward Black and Latinx people and other people of color that has profoundly limited their educational opportunities (p. 9). The resulting educational debt is not something that children can overcome if they simply try hard enough or believe that they have the potential for growth. The root of the problem is not the individual; rather it is the system that reproduces and reifies oppression.

"Bootstrap" frameworks like grit and growth mindset are problematic because they are devoid of a critical analysis that would shift the gaze from the individual students or teachers to the systems and structures that perpetuate inequities (Anyon, 1980; Payne, 2008; Shedd, 2015; Willis, 1981). The underlying premise with these frameworks is that all things are equal, when they are not. Leaders who demand excellence without working to dismantle oppressive structures that reproduce inequity are practicing limiting care because they lack an understanding and critique of structural oppression.

High-Stakes Testing and Accountability Policies

Frequently, when conversations about student and teacher excellence arise, the narrative shifts to a focus on increasing testing to hold both accountable. Radical care in leadership focuses on seeing and building capacity for excellence, but that should not be confused with the accountability rhetoric and practices that have historically dominated educational discourse in this country (Kamenetz, 2015; Ravitch, 2013). Although the testing rhetoric is often framed as a way to close so-called "achievement gaps" between Whites and Blacks and other minoritized groups, testing policies have historically been designed to reinforce these inequities, not remedy them (Au, 2008, 2016). Far from improving outcomes for Black and Latinx students, the hyperfocus on testing has had a harmful impact on their outcomes (Amrein & Berliner, 2003, 2008; Au, 2011; Vasquez Heilig & Darling-Hammond, 2008). While Whiter and more affluent school districts have been able to maintain educational integrity and innovation, already underresourced schools who serve predominantly Black and Latinx students have decreased or eliminated subjects and learning experiences that are not measured by a standardized assessment.

These kinds of accountability policies, which are falsely conflated with excellence, encourage leaders to practice limiting care because they are focused on increasing test scores at all costs, typically at the expense of Black and Latinx students' actual success. This is not at all a vision of excellence that is in alignment with radical care. Rather, it is a form of limiting care, because it focuses on asking students and teachers to do more than what is reasonable or beneficial given the limited resources they have been given. The goal should not be to set the bar higher and higher, then ask teachers to get students to soar over that bar without providing the supports and resources to meet those standards. Unfortunately, federal, state, and local accountability policies tend to define achievement in this way, focusing on academic gaps without thoughtfully addressing opportunity gaps that create disparate achievement outcomes (Au, 2008; Ravitch, 2013). This is a perfect example of demanding more without providing the scaffolds and supports students need to successfully meet those demands. Too frequently, schools fail to provide the resources that help bridge gaps. Simply expecting more, without providing the resources for students to catch up is problematic and antithetical to radical care.

BELIEVING IN STUDENTS' AND TEACHERS' CAPACITY FOR EXCELLENCE IN PRACTICE

At Innovation High School in the Bronx, principal Miriam Samuel was managing a major transition from high-stakes standardized tests to performance-based assessment tasks (PBATs). As a new member in the New York Performance Assessment Consortium, teachers and students had to shift their approaches to teaching and learning. There were significant growing pains as perceptions about what assessment should and could look like were challenged. However, the school already had a history of cultivating authentic relationships, so the difficult conversations about standards and expectations were able to unfold as needed. In one meeting I observed, Samuel encouraged the teachers to reflect, "What do you need to prep kids in the 9th grade for PBATs? From 10th to 11th to 12th? Forget the time, the space, the logistics. Figure out what we need, then we'll manage all the rest." By telling the teachers to ignore the sticky questions around the how, Samuel gave them space to take risks and consider what was possible. At the same time, Samuel was pushing them to deepen their capacity for imagining educational excellence for their students.

By clearly signaling to the teachers that she believed they were capable of excellence, Samuel also conveyed the same mindset about the students. And, indeed, I observed the teachers explicitly grappling with what it meant to honor students' process and effort without compromising on their expectations for student excellence. In meetings, staff members debated this issue, with some teachers explicitly raising questions of race and lowered expectations for students of color. These deliberations carried into students' PBAT presentation, with teachers explicitly engaging students in conversations about excellence. An excerpt from my field notes of the conversation teachers had with one senior following her English Language Arts PBAT presentation:

Teacher 1: I'd love to give everyone a "Competent," but we can't pass them to assuage their feelings.

Student is asking what she means.

Teacher 2: Your panel feels that you have the capacity to do much better.

Teacher 1: I wouldn't be able to sleep at night if I told you this was competent. It would be a disservice.

The student nods her head in understanding.

Teacher 2: It is a measure of your maturity that you're not defensive. My concern is that we're lowering standards [if we pass you].

Here, the teachers engaged honestly with the student about their obligation to hold her to high standards. They acknowledged their ethical responsibility to demand excellence. Failing to pass the PBAT at that moment in time did not preclude the student from revising the task and working to her full potential. After this exchange, the teachers explicitly discussed with the student how she could improve her work to pass the PBAT, and what supports they would provide her. In this observation and others, the message was clear: Failure led to greater opportunities to learn.

At School for Social Justice, Bronx middle school principal Byron Johnson actively sought out new knowledge about all things education and jumped at opportunities to push the boundaries of what is possible in public education. He visited public and independent schools locally and in other states to find innovative practices that he might adopt at SFSJ. He was not afraid to experiment with these new ideas nor did he shy away from the potential logistical challenges, such as scheduling, that might arise from innovating. Most importantly, his belief in the capacity to learn and grow was not limited to himself. He believed it of his staff, and he believed it of his students. In pushing his teachers to rise to excellence, he was cultivating a culture of excellence for SFSJ students, as well. This underlying belief drove his leadership practice.

Johnson frequently engaged in conversation with other educators, virtually and face-to-face, who were also interested in exploring problems of practice, such as debating the value of homework, for continuous learning and growth. This was a highly reflective stance and it informed Johnson's daily leadership practice in the school. Indeed, a key feature of his leadership practice involved expecting his faculty to also be reflective and to consider how they might change education for the betterment of all of their students.

Johnson pushed his staff to create learning experiences for students that went beyond the traditional paradigms of education. Given the increased standardization of education and teaching, with the proliferation of accountability mandates that have had a chilling effect on ingenuity and innovation (Baker, 2012), Johnson's message to his teachers pushed back on this trend and aimed to redirect their energies. Rather than default to the traditional "drill and kill" paradigm that were part of the practice of many schools serving communities similar to SFSJ, Johnson's emphasis was on encouraging teachers to focus on developing authentic and engaging learning practices that promoted the development of critical thinking skills. In one of his bulletins, he wrote,

> I need for all of us, the entire staff, to become visionaries. To become thought leaders and design thinkers regarding the world around us. I need for all of us to reimagine school, community, and society as we see fit. Media and peers have programmed us to focus on what's wrong in society and become stagnated in the "what" and "why" of the world. Constantly asking others to give us things. We must mobilize, relentlessly, individually and collectively, toward making sense of and understanding big ideas so that we can create what we need. Our kids and community need it more than ever, and we must lead them. (November 16, 2015)

Recognizing that test preparation would not yield excellent teaching and learning, nor would it create rigorous and high expectations for the students, Johnson eschewed test prep and messaged the value of reflection and growth in his bulletins.

Johnson was not unconcerned with students progressing from grade to grade; rather, he was more concerned with the individual life chances of students and with the overall improvement of the status of his Black and Latinx students. Here, his administrator responsibilities were tempered by what Lomotey (1993) described as an "ethno-humanist" role, or the personal connections to the needs of students beyond the bureaucratic demands. Johnson's approach was an embodiment of radical care in that he was less concerned with propping up a testing policy that was actually harmful to students of color; he was fiercely protective of their opportunities to learn authentically.

When, in spring 2014, the NYC Schools Chancellor mandated that elementary and middle schools develop alternative promotional criteria based on student portfolios in response to the growing discontent around the state exams, Johnson seized the opportunity to encourage his staff to teach with a different goal in mind. He wrote in his bulletin, "We now have the freedom to truly meet students where they are and consistently teach and assess the 21st-century skills our students will need to be happy and productive global citizens" (April 14, 2014). Rather than being hyperfocused on test performance, Johnson encouraged his staff to take advantage of the new policy and create educational tasks that both addressed individualized student learning needs and provided them with necessary skills for future success. Here, he pushed staff to do right by the children, creating a caring climate that addressed the students' need to be prepared for the world beyond SFSJ. In response to some pushback he received from teachers regarding these changes, Johnson argued, "What I'm hearing is 'the test, the test.' That will keep us bogged down! These are opportunities to be awesome!"

After the meeting, Johnson reflected on the resistance that surfaced and decided that he needed to provide substantive and meaningful resources to help teachers make the shift and become exemplary. Johnson understood that he needed to actively support teachers in order to help the students achieve success. He admitted to me that he was beginning to recognize that encouragement alone was insufficient. Johnson's support for teachers went beyond the tangible resource provisions, however. A large part of how he supported their growth was through his own transparent risk-taking and reflection. Weekly "Johnson Bulletins" and other communications shared with staff typically included examples of how Johnson liked to think through tough ideas. In the November 16, 2015 bulletin, for instance, he explicitly pushed his staff to be reflective and consistently improving their practice, and further listed some strategies he used to further his thinking. He wrote:

> What I'm strongly encouraging first and foremost is for us to be reflective. Reflect on our daily practice, reflect on our pedagogy, and reflect on our mindset. Am I a "yes and" person or a "yeah but"

person? Have I internalized a growth mindset? If so, how do I maintain it? If not, how do I get there? Blogging/writing is a great reflective tool and very therapeutic. Staff needs to push each other toward these ideas, so that we can skyrocket toward transforming education as we know it.

Johnson pushed the staff to reflect on the extent to which they were open to possibilities. He also expected his staff to push each other to excel and to constantly reflect on their practice. In essence, he expected them to lift each other as they climbed.

A critical component in his leadership was that he did, in fact, expect his teachers to be reflective, to try to grow as pedagogues. Johnson took a "no excuses" stance when it came to this. In one communication to the staff, he wrote,

Mediocrity is totally unacceptable. You all are too capable for that! Master the Danielson [evaluation] rubric and leverage your colleagues and your union for support. Build your professional learning network outside of school. Excuses and blame are dead in our school. (June 15, 2014)

Although this language is tough, embedded within it was Johnson's belief that everyone, including his teaching staff, had the capacity for excellence. This communication was not intended to be punitive; rather, it was an emphatic declaration that after a year of adjusting to a new teacher evaluation tool, Johnson believed that teachers were ready to be pushed to their growing edge. His motivation was to inspire his teachers to excel in their practice. As he further explained in the bulletin, "The only way for us to be our best is if I push you to be your best." Johnson's view was that if he did his job well, the staff would lead themselves, and each other, to high standards of practice. This, Johnson believed, would lead to growth and excellence for students, as well.

The founding school leader at Bridges Institute, Jeff Wagner, also pushed teachers to have high standards of practice for themselves and their students. He frequently reminded the teachers that they must teach up to students, because students are more capable of standards of excellence than those to which they were being held. After his retirement in 1996, he wrote the following in a letter to the staff:

Students need to get into the regular habit of doing work and being held accountable for it. . . . We should teach up to our students. They

are capable of doing more than they (or in some cases we) can imagine. We cannot afford to allow students to "get away" with not doing
their work. There are effective ways to deal with this, but we have
to be persistent and tough enough to carry them out, whether that
means keeping students after class, bringing them in early, keeping
the building open, with supervision, until 5 p.m. every day, holding
regular family conferences, or whatever.

Wagner was calling out teachers for having lowered their expectations for their students, probably unconsciously, and, in so doing, he also
communicated that he expected excellence from the teachers. He made
it clear that they had to do whatever it took to ensure that kids could
reach the potential that the kids themselves might not have imagined they
could reach.

CONCLUSION

Believing that our students and teachers are capable of excellence requires
an active rejection of the persistent narrative that the trajectories of teachers and students are predetermined by the circumstances of their context.
And yet, this false narrative is seemingly bolstered when Black and Latinx
communities are labeled "failing" without a real analysis of the structural
oppression that has failed those same communities. Rather than blaming
teachers and students for limitations, leaders who practice radical care
understand that they are responsible for providing the resources and supports that are essential to support opportunities for teachers and students
to continuously strive for and achieve excellence. To demand excellence,
they must also have cultivated authentic relationships with teachers, students, and their families.

Leaders who practice radical care also understand how to strategically
leverage power to create conditions where believing in the capacity for
excellence is possible. This includes using their authority to transform internal school systems and routines so that they are more responsive to the
needs of their school community. It might also include activating allies to
resist policies, like high-stakes testing, that are antithetical to radical care.
Finally, it might include taking a personal and public stand against injustice. I explore the importance of strategically leveraging power in greater
detail in the following chapter.

CHAPTER 4

Component 4
Leveraging Power Strategically

> Every year in my children's former elementary school, 3rd-graders put on a musical puppet show that focuses on a historical event directed by a theater company in residence. The year my 3rd-grader participated, the focus of the musical was Henry Hudson. As was customary in the school, the principal introduced the performance to the parents, expressing her admiration for the teachers' and students' hard work and creativity. The show began and the kids, dressed in black, masterfully managed life-size puppets and sang songs chronicling Henry Hudson's voyages. At first impressed by the artistry, my emotions quickly shifted to shock and outrage when, as the kids started to sing about Hudson's interactions with Indigenous people, I realized that the refrain involved frequent use of the word "savages." I came to learn that, earlier that day, these students had also performed the show for all of the other children in grades K–5.

In the vignette, the school's principal did no more than introduce the performance by praising all of those involved with the show. The show's program listed the names of all participants and the title of performance. There was no context or discussion about historical representations and narratives. There was also no indication that the principal had provided a framing for the other children in the school who had seen the show earlier that day. Not only were the 3rd-graders performing this tune, it was possible that other kids in the school were also now mindlessly humming or singing the song's refrain, unconsciously repeating the racist slur without any kind of critical understanding about the pain and trauma associated with that word throughout history.

There was no direct or indirect explanation of the contested and violent history of European exploration in the Americas. There were no links directing audience members where they might go for an accurate representation of the history or even any acknowledgment that the representation of Hudson's journey would reinforce a White supremacist narrative.

This vignette highlights a seemingly benign acceptance of a beloved tradition and ritual within a school that lacks a critical examination of how it serves to reinforce hegemony and inequality. This is a failure on the part of the leader to strategically leverage their power to interrogate and disrupt a tradition that was actually quite harmful and destructive. By failing to take any of these steps to address the reinforcement of racist tropes and ideologies, the leader was practicing limiting care.

The fourth component of radical care focuses specifically on the importance of the leader as a change agent who understands the power they have and is strategic about how they leverage it to improve education for the communities they serve. Had the leader in this vignette practiced radical care, it is likely that this play would not even have been selected for performance. If, however, the principal first became aware of the content of the play after the performance had already taken place, she would have leveraged her power to create spaces for educators to reflect on the messages the play conveyed. This would have extended beyond this individual play; indeed, these conversations would be springboards for further critical analysis of curricular content. The school leader who practices radical care might have also used the performance as an opportunity to create a powerful learning experience for students to learn about Hudson's exploration with a more critical lens.

To be certain, disruptions of the sort I'm suggesting require the leader to understand the importance of strategically using their power in the school, not to unilaterally mandate change, but rather to engage the community in a process of transformation. Of course, there is always the potential for significant pushback when beloved rituals are disrupted. Leaders who practice radical care understand that the relationships discussed in Chapter 2 make it possible to create spaces within their school communities for difficult conversations wherein educators can be engaged in a process of reflecting on harmful practices that have been taken for granted. Leaders who practice radical care lean into this challenge because it is a moral imperative to engage in antiracist practices.

WHAT IT MEANS TO STRATEGICALLY LEVERAGE POWER

The fourth component of radical care focuses specifically on the importance of the leader as a change agent who navigates challenging contexts while skillfully leading within the school community. The key here is that the leader who practices radical care is strategic; they are thoughtful about how to leverage their positional authority to engage with other

educators on their staff, as well as community members and the broader
public, with the goals of equity and racial justice in mind. That is not to
say that the power is weaponized; rather, the leader practicing radical care
considers how their power can be exercised in thoughtful ways to enact
changes that will advance racial justice and equity. These leaders thoughtfully examine longstanding practices or traditions within the school, as
well as externally imposed policies, to determine if their impact will cause
their students harm. Such leaders know that challenging harmful internal
or external policies is a moral imperative and an essential part of a framework of radical care. This is made possible because these school leaders
understand the full picture of the sociopolitical context in which their
school and the community are situated, and they leverage their power in
those broader contexts as well. Although there are numerous ways leaders can leverage their power, these strategies can be organized into three
broad characteristics: (1) challenging the institutional norms within the
school, (2) challenging harmful policies, and (3) taking a public stance
against injustice.

First, leaders who practice radical care use their power to challenge assumptions about the way their schools are organized. So often in schools,
we reproduce practices—such as teacher assignment, textbook selection,
or student tracking, among other norms—without a second thought simply because "that's just how it's always been done." Absent from that sentiment is thoughtful consideration of how the practices actually impact
students and the community. These are practices that are handed down
and accepted because no one is challenging the value of continuing certain institutional routines and practices. Often, a closer look at some of
these practices and norms that have become habitual reveals that they are
not actually benefiting all kids.

Leaders who practice radical care understand that their positional
authority allows them to thoughtfully engage the school community in
interrogating—and disrupting, if necessary—practices that are not in the
best interests of creating high-quality learning opportunities for Black
and Latinx students. Leaders who are committed to practicing radical
care have engaged with their community to understand institutional oppression and, as a result, they are primed for rejecting the traditional way
of doing things when those ways have a negative impact on their communities. Having higher expectations for staff and students, by encouraging
innovation and excellence, is not without risk because it represents a challenge to the status quo. This is why leaders practicing radical care must
leverage their power strategically, ensuring that they are cognizant about
how and when they push against these internal norms.

A second characteristic of leaders who strategically leverage power is understanding their responsibility to push back on externally imposed policies that are going to be harmful to their students. Being able to strategically navigate a volatile bureaucratic landscape without losing sight of a vision of schooling that is grounded in antiracism (Dantley, 2009; Lomotey, 1993) is essential for leaders practicing radical care. Again, the strategic nature of this work is critical, because resisting harmful policies can leave leaders in a vulnerable position. Advocating on behalf of students and school communities may be unpopular with policymakers or other superiors, putting school leaders who practice radical care at risk. If, after the leader evaluates a policy and determines that noncompliance or some other form of resistance is in order, the school leader has to determine when and how to resist. In some cases, this kind of leadership work must be subversive, and the leader has to strategically activate allies to advocate on behalf of the school as the leader's proxies (Siddle Walker, 2018). In order to navigate this challenge successfully, these leaders lean on their strong communities of allies who value the leader's expertise and discernment. To do this, they have to cultivate a broad base of allies, but this cannot happen if the school leader has not worked to develop strong authentic relationships that are grounded in trust and understanding (Young et al., 2015).

Finally, leaders who practice radical care and leverage their power strategically understand that there are times when they must be front and center, publicly taking a stand against injustices (Bogotch, 2002; Jean-Marie et al., 2009; Rivera-McCutchen, 2014; Theoharis, 2009). By engaging in public forms of activism, leaders not only leverage their power and positional authority to bring attention to an issue, but their actions also serve as a model for educators, students, and the broader community. They engage forcefully and publicly and, in so doing, also work to catalyze change. They understand the political and revolutionary nature of education (Kirylo, 2017; Lanas & Zembylas, 2015), and leaders who practice radical care work actively and publicly to advocate against structural oppression in all forms.

Radical care involves leaders explicitly calling out institutional racism in ways that are highly politicized by virtue of their public nature. They leverage their positional authority to elevate their advocacy against oppression using platforms (i.e., blogs, public statements posted online, letters to the editor, comments to the press, and so on) that amplify their message in ways that connect with broader audiences (Rivera-McCutchen, 2019). Rather than concentrating their efforts solely on their individual school communities, raising their activism to a more public level has the potential to increase their impact on other communities. Doing so raises their profile, however, and puts them at real risk of retaliation and hyperscrutiny by the very power structures they are critiquing.

CONDITIONS FOR LEVERAGING POWER STRATEGICALLY

Leaders who engage in radical care practices understand the importance of leveraging power strategically in order to organize for change, which cannot happen in isolation from the other components of radical care. First, school leaders must understand the full picture of the sociopolitical context in which their school is situated (Curry, 2016; Rivera-McCutchen, 2021). Leaders practicing radical care understand that policies, practices, and norms, inside and outside of their schools, have been shaped by oppressive systems that reinforce inequity, especially for Black and Latinx students. Their antiracist stance shapes the leader's analysis of how social and educational policies impact the communities they serve, and how access to institutions (educational or otherwise) are shaped and/or constrained by the enactment of those policies. Accordingly, leaders practicing radical care leverage their power and strategically organize all aspects of their schools to resist systemic and institutional oppression and racism (Antrop-González & De Jesús, 2006).

Being able to strategically navigate a volatile bureaucratic landscape without losing sight of a vision of schooling that is grounded in antiracism and social justice (Dantley, 2009; Lomotey, 1993) is another essential aspect of radical care. They must navigate the policy contexts in order to determine how best to comply with the spirit of the law while not putting their school in harm's way (Gooden & Dantley, 2012). As Lomotey (1993) noted, principals must move fluidly between their roles as bureaucratic administrators and ethnohumanists in order to make decisions about policy that are best for the community they serve. Johnson's example of both administering the state assessments, while also being outspoken about the limits of the tests are an example of navigating both of these roles. This "double-consciousness" (Dantley, 2009) is a critical skill displayed by school leaders practicing radical care.

Part of leveraging power strategically is discerning the most effective approach to creating change to existing policies and routines. In all cases, changes require cultivating authentic relationships in order to engage in conversations about the transformation that is needed. When it comes to reforming internal processes, relationships prove to be an essential factor because change requires a willingness to take risks and trust in the person leading the change. Leaders have to be able to engage teachers and students in change processes, as well as to engage parents and community members as allies. Leveraging power is not intended to suggest a strong-armed approach. Rather, it positions the school leader to utilize their privileged position as the leader to create opportunities for meaningful collaboration with others. Part of leveraging power is building the capacity among teachers and staff to ensure that leadership is continuous and that engaging with and for communities becomes part of the ethos of the school. Leaders who practice radical care believe that the students and teachers are capable of excellence were it not for barriers that reproduce institutional oppression. It is this firm belief that fuels their commitment to leveraging their power to create opportunities where all members of the school community can meet and exceed their potential.

Finally, leaders who adopt a radical care framework firmly believe that transformation is possible. They enact their power out of a moral sense of obligation to address wrongs (Rivera-McCutchen, 2014). They believe that the risks involved with agitating for transformation within the school and in the broader context will pay off. These leaders are spurred on by a moral imperative to engage vigorously in the struggle for equality despite the perils of so doing.

FAILING TO STRATEGICALLY LEVERAGE POWER

While school leaders have positional authority, holding the role of principal alone is not an adequate lever for transformation. Maintaining the status quo will do more to perpetuate institutional oppression than dismantle it. Without disrupting internal processes or advocating for change in policies, there is little opportunity for students and teachers to fulfill their capacity for excellence. One example of a widespread practice that can often be problematic is teacher assignment, a practice that is frequently unchanged. There is an unspoken understanding in many schools that veteran teachers get to teach classes that are considered to be more attractive. These might be honors classes or gifted classes. Yet the research is pretty clear that, generally speaking, assigning the most experienced and highly qualified teachers to teach students who need the most academic support is good practice (Cardichon et al, 2020; Darling-Hammond, 2010). School leaders who fail to challenge these procedures are practicing a form of limiting care because their emphasis is on maintaining practices that will cause the least amount of resistance.

These school-level policies that reinforce oppression are bolstered by local, state, and national policies that fail to prioritize teacher preparation and assignments that would address inequitable access to highly qualified educators. Programs like Teach for America, which fast-track certification and place novice and underqualified educators in schools where students have historically received inferior education, have a tendency to reinforce limiting care practices that uphold structures that are oppressive rather than liberating for Black and Latinx students and other students of color.

STRATEGICALLY LEVERAGING POWER IN ACTION

One of the significant challenges school leaders may face is the need to balance their responses to policy demands and mandates while also determining how those demands align with the best interests of the community. Frequently, the problematic school policies arise from racist structures and work to reinforce and deepen inequities. Given the structures that reproduce inequality in predictable patterns, school leaders who are committed to radical care strategically leverage their power in an effort to transform schools and society. School leaders who practice radical care see themselves as change agents who navigate the external context while skillfully leading within the school community (Khalifa, 2012; Lomotey, 1993).

Challenging Institutional Norms

At SFSJ, for example, Bronx middle school principal Byron Johnson took the bold step to completely disrupt the traditional scheduling and began to innovate. While most school leaders wouldn't dare touch the schedule, Johnson knew that students were struggling in literacy and also that constructivist pedagogical approaches and design-thinking were better than "drill and kill." However, to make this change required skillful leadership that was strategic in assessing the potential impact of this change not just on students, but also on teachers.

When Johnson first introduced the idea at a staff meeting, many of the teachers were reticent. However, Johnson had cultivated a school climate where the teachers felt free to express their concerns. This was not complaining; rather, they expressed their resistance in ways that suggested that dialogue and disagreement were part of the professional culture. This was a result of the relationships Johnson developed in the school. They trusted his leadership and took a risk, despite many of their concerns because they understood that Johnson would support them, but most importantly, they understood that, as a result of his leadership, the change could be better for the students. As a result, the school's schedule was changed so that students could have two 60-minute "Genius Hour" blocks, where they worked on projects of their choosing and interest. That eventually evolved into an entrepreneurship class and electives. Focusing on the "whole child" rather than on test prep seems to have paid off, with students' test scores remaining generally higher than their peer group across the Bronx.

Since Johnson viewed the education landscape as full of possibilities for liberation of marginalized communities, he was less inclined to feel constrained by policy and context than others might. He navigated the political and policy landscape strategically and deftly while at the same time not sacrificing his ideals. When I asked him how educational policy impacts his leadership, Johnson chuckled and responded, "policy doesn't drive my behavior." He further explained,

> I look at policy in terms of mandates and compliance. What do I need to do to make sure I am in compliance and what do I need to do to make sure I'm meeting all the mandates? Other than that, I follow my experience and my heart and my common sense. . . . There have been times where we have bagged some of the policy that's *bestowed* [Johnson is chuckling] upon us to get certain things accomplished. We've been creative in stretching the letter of the law. We work more with the spirit of the law than the letter of the law. (B. Johnson, personal communication, February 17, 2014)

Rather than comply without question, Johnson's comments suggest that his decisionmaking around policy implementation within his school was guided first and foremost by the well-being of his students.

Challenging Harmful Policies

When creatively working around policy is not possible, school leaders who practice radical care strategically engage allies, leveraging their power skillfully. For example, at Bridges Institute, former high school principal Michael Warren told me a couple of stories about Mothers on the Move (MOM), a powerful grassroots South Bronx organization whose mission was to reform public schools in their neighborhoods. In 1995, after NYC schools' chancellor Ramon Cortines backed out of a meeting with MOM, 50 of their members went to Cortines's home in Brooklyn, generating bad press for him.

Several of the MOM's children were students at the Bridges Institute. Rather than see MOM as adversarial, Warren viewed them as allies. So, when the superintendent planned to significantly increase the school's enrollment, Warren mobilized MOM among others and said, "I need phone calls to the superintendent. . . . Somebody needs to read him the riot act about what's going to happen to the superintendency if we get all these extra kids." He encouraged them to be as tough as possible, but strategically added, "Don't tell him I told you to call." Warren knew that, politically, he could not afford to directly confront the superintendent. However, he correctly assessed that powerful outside allies, such as Mothers on the Move, could apply enough pressure on behalf of the school. Warren understood that it was a moral imperative to act and he leveraged his power to successful resist a policy change that would negatively impact his students.

Responding to Injustice

In other cases, the resistance must be public, where the school leader is deliberately and actively in the public eye advocating for a cause that impacts their students and others as well. On the morning after a grand jury refused to indict the Ferguson police officer who killed Michael Brown, Byron Johnson invited interested students and fellow staff who were outraged to participate in a march to protest the decision. Radical care demands that leaders take a principled and visible stand against racism and other injustices. There can be no ambiguities.

Leveraging Power Strategically:
Overlap of Internal and External Resistance

There are times when leaders who practice radical care leverage their power in ways that the three characteristics I described earlier overlap. That is to say that there are internal disruptions to norms that the leader undertakes, while also engaging allies to disrupt systemic-level policies in highly publicized ways. One example of this was principal Byron Johnson's resistance against high-stakes testing. After experiencing a growing frustration with how the New York State standardized tests were constraining curriculum and draining resources, Johnson began navigating the tension between policy demands and socially just practice. Johnson understood that testing policies were deeply flawed and also had a particularly negative impact on Black and Latinx students' academic outcomes.

First, he began making curricular and structural changes within his school, challenging the institutional norms that had historically focused on test prep. He pushed teachers to be innovative in their curricular choices and reject the tendency to engage in "drill and kill" teaching approaches. Since teacher evaluations were tied to test results, he engaged in ongoing conversations with teachers to support their development around understanding that teaching to the test did not benefit students. He frequently and passionately cited the disparities in both resource distribution between schools like SFSJ when compared to private, mostly White schools as a byproduct of structural racism. Because of the authentic relationships he cultivated within the school community, coupled with a longstanding schoolwide commitment to antiracism, Johnson was able to have thoughtful conversations about moving away from test-prep and the challenges involved with the curricular innovation. Having created a culture where excellence was expected, the conversations around innovation also centered on the potential for student and teacher growth.

At the same time that these internal conversations were happening, Johnson was also working with the parent association at his school to inform them of their rights to opt out of the standardized tests. These conversations represented an effort to exert pressure on a systemic testing policy that had increasingly stifled curriculum and limited opportunities for exploration and innovation in schools primarily attended by Black and Latinx students. By engaging parents in this effort, Johnson was strategically leveraging his power and the relationships he had cultivated to push for transformation. However, as the opt-out efforts began to gain traction across the city and state, NYC school leaders were discouraged from publicizing the opportunities for parents to opt their children out of the exams (deMause, 2016). Subsequently, Johnson's efforts in the "opt-out" movement became more public and, just before the 2015–2016 school year, he authored a blog post about the "tyranny" of testing, comparing high-stakes standardized testing to modern-day slavery. Arguing that the tests deepened inequities, Johnson forcefully advocated for structural change that would transform public education into places where students of color would have unfettered access to excellent education. Here, Johnson leveraged his power to draw attention to a testing policy he deemed to be flawed, and he drew parallels between the impact of testing and test prep with other kinds of physical and emotional violence in communities of color. This was a stance that fueled his work inside and outside the school.

Over the next several years, Johnson crisscrossed New York State speaking to community members who were interested in learning more about opting their children out of the tests. Moreover, in contributions to local and national media outlets, Johnson expanded his critique of the assessments and connected the dots between the tests and the divestment in public education in the state, particularly for Black and Latinx communities. Specifically, Johnson directly challenged Success Academy Charter network and others that overemphasized testing at the expense of students' opportunities to explore engaging curriculum. Instead, Johnson argued, children in schools should have the opportunity to be design-thinkers and innovators, a learning approach that can be discouraged by a high-stakes accountability environment.

Despite the clear warnings from the NYC Department of Education, Johnson persisted in his public activism and worked alongside activists in the statewide grassroots opt-out organization, the New York State Alliance for Public Education, regularly lending his voice to press releases aimed at changing testing policies. While Johnson also made structural and curricular changes in his school to address some of his concerns, as described above, his public advocacy was on behalf of all Black and Latinx students negatively impacted by high-stakes accountability policies. Johnson's activism at the city and state levels explicitly challenged structural racism and contributed to increase numbers of Black and Latinx parents opting their children out of the New York State exams. It likely also contributed to the New York State Board of Regents' softening of their approach to standardized testing in grades 3–8 by decreasing the length of the tests, and also placing a moratorium on the use of the assessment results for teacher evaluations.

Johnson's actions aligned with the important leadership principle of navigating a political and policy landscape nimbly (Lomotey, 1993), while at the same time refusing to sacrifice his ideals. Johnson's resistance and activism aimed to protect his students, and all students, from the harm of misguided and dangerous education policy. Like scholar Asa Hilliard III (as cited in Tillman, 2008), Johnson believed that high-stakes tests are not "an innocent school improvement activity" (p. 595). Like IQ testing, Johnson saw them as a major barrier for schools and, like Hilliard, as the "enemy of millions of children who have unrecognized genius" (as cited in Tillman, 2008, p. 595). This belief disallowed him from silently accepting a flawed accountability policy that harmed his students.

CONCLUSION

School leaders' positional authority grants them a degree of power that they leverage strategically if they are practicing radical care. This is not a megalomaniacal power use; rather, it is borne out of a deep sense of commitment to the goals of equity and liberation. Their use of power is grounded in authentic relationships and a desire to disrupt oppressive policies in structures. As the examples in the chapter illuminate, leaders practicing radical care must earn the trust of teachers, staff, students, and their families and work collaboratively with them to successfully advocate for the benefit of all members of the school community.

Leaders who practice radical care understand that there is a great deal of risk involved in working to dismantle oppressive systems, and yet they see themselves as duty-bound to fight for educational equality and justice. They must be vigilant in examining seemingly race-neutral policies (López, 2003) that are in fact deliberate efforts to disenfranchise communities of color. Finally, leading with radical care involves being pragmatic in how and when resistance should take shape.

CHAPTER 5

Component 5
Embracing a Spirit of Radical Hope

> At a local town hall for students in my community in fall 2020, several students talked about the isolation they were feeling while learning remotely during the COVID-19 pandemic, and the pressure of being required to engage in synchronous online instruction every day. Students talked about the increasing workload and wondered if the teachers realized that they were assigning far more work than they would if school were in person. Students lamented their lack of connection to their peers and teachers. Some of the students talked about their need to work during the day to support their families, while others talked about missing their classes because they needed to help their younger siblings with online school. One student shared, and others agreed, that she didn't feel like she was attending school to learn. Rather, she was in school to submit her assignments in Google classroom by 11:59 p.m.

At the onset of the pandemic in spring 2020, there was widespread confusion about how to manage the sometimes competing needs of teachers, students, and their families. Compounding this issue was the uncertainty regarding the length of time the disruption would last. States across the country canceled standardized exams (Gottlieb & Schneider, 2020), and in many schools educators were encouraged to spend significant time checking in on students' socioemotional well-being. Rather than try to make school continue with "business as usual," there was general consensus that, as a society, we needed to get everyone to the end of the school year. And yet, as the vignette suggests, once school resumed in the fall, the rhetoric around schooling shifted to refocus on rigor, standards, and accountability, without an equally strong narrative around how students', families', and educators' basic emotional and human needs were being met. Rather than seeing the opportunity that emerged from the disruption of schooling as usual, many leaders defaulted to their normal way of operating and planning for the worst. Complacently accepting the inevitability of failure in the face of this pandemic, especially for Black and Latinx communities, is unacceptable. Limiting care, in this vignette, takes shape in the form of acknowledging the disparities that the pandemic is deepening, without committing to forceful action to harness the moment to disrupt the inequities.

Embracing a spirit of radical hope, the fifth component of a framework of radical care, demands that leaders see challenges as opportunities for transformation. To say that COVID-19 will impact a generation of children is an understatement. However, leaders who practice radical care see and fight for possibilities in this moment of upheaval (Roy, 2020). As Bettina Love (2020) highlighted in a panel discussion late in spring 2020 after the start of the pandemic, amazing things happened when schools physically shut down. She notes that, in many urban school districts, one-to-one access to laptops had been thought to be an impossibility, and yet, once schools closed and the traditional paradigms were disrupted, devices were distributed to students. Free internet was made available to families, and other critical educational resources that were previously inaccessible, especially for low-income communities of color, were made available. While these efforts were not without limitations, wider access to material resources that was previously thought impossible was made possible. Embracing a spirit of radical hope, then, is working against seemingly insurmountable challenges and resisting the temptation to complacently accept the conditions that are normally present. It is believing that we can achieve the impossible.

WHAT IS RADICAL HOPE?

Hope in the face of trauma and hardship is essential to the work of radical care in leadership. Too often, our schools are underresourced, as are the communities they serve. The challenges of addressing institutional oppression at times seem insurmountable; it is essential, then, that the school leader maintain a level of intense and almost unbelievable optimism if they are to effectively lead. Embracing a spirit of radical hope, the final component of radical care, is marked by two characteristics: (1) seeing challenges as opportunities and (2) energizing others around doing the same. Radical hope is the spirit that enables the school leader to energize themselves and the communities they lead. It empowers them to believe that change and betterment is possible, and that the risks they take to lead their school communities will ultimately lead to improved outcomes for the students they serve. As Robin D. G. Kelley (2002) reminds us in his powerful book, *Freedom Dreams,* "unless we have the space to imagine and a vision of what it means fully to realize our humanity, all the protests and demonstrations in the world won't bring about our liberation" (p. 198).

Leaders who embrace a spirit of radical hope guard themselves against the despair (Díaz, 2016) that is hard to avoid when working within systems that are so deeply inequitable and entrenched. However, radical hope should not be confused with a false or passive optimism. Radical hope is active and agentic and involves having faith that struggles for justice will prevail. It is a commitment to persistently confront inequity. Conversely, a leader who practices limiting care may acknowledge structural oppression and believe that changes should be made, but may choose not to engage in the active efforts to dismantle systems that reproduce inequities. Passive optimism and hope are forms of limiting care because they cede power and agency.

Embracing a spirit of radical hope is not about deluding oneself; leaders who engage in this work are honest about the institutional oppression that shapes the educational experiences of children of color. So, false optimism is not possible for these leaders. They have seen too much to be deluded. Rather, radical hope is the ardent belief in what is possible, given the commitment to the struggle for liberation. It is rooted in a profound understanding that theirs is the work of generations. Justice and freedom are not achieved overnight or even in one generation. There is progress, then loss, and still the struggle must continue. Radical hope lives in that space—there is something truly prophetic about it.

CONDITIONS THAT FOSTER RADICAL HOPE

Embracing a spirit of radical hope is integrally connected to the first four components of radical care that have been discussed in detail throughout this book. Radical hope grows out of an understanding that structural oppression is manifested in schools and the communities they serve. The word "radical" in front of hope, necessarily implies that those who embrace it must have a clear and critical understanding of how antiracism is a fundamental part of dismantling and reimagining oppressive educational institutions. Leaders who embrace a spirit of radical hope understand that though systems are oppressive, they are not deterministic (Ginwright, 2016; Green, 2016; Miller et al., 2011).

In order to embrace radical hope and move toward action, leaders must work alongside their communities, forging authentic relationships that are reciprocal, and grounded in a fundamental valuing and desiring of what others bring to the school. Leaders who embrace this ethic "go to the people humbly, openly, and ready to listen to their ideas" (Miller et al., 2011, p. 1082). Through these relationships and trust building, leaders who embrace a spirit of radical hope cultivate a shared sense of purpose, energy, and agency that motivates all to act toward a possible future (Duncan-Andrade, 2009).

The belief in students' and teachers' capacity to achieve excellence is also dependent upon a spirit of radical hope that imagines what is possible to achieve. It is grounded in an explicit rejection of complacency or, more specifically, a rejection of deficit beliefs of people, which discourage work and efforts for improvement and work toward an imagined potential. Rather, leaders who embrace a spirit of radical hope insist that we ask again and again, "What could be?" To be clear, this should not be confused with false hope (Duncan-Andrade, 2009) or passive optimism. It is not a lazy belief that if we just hope for something long enough or hard enough, it will come true. Fundamentally, radical hope is a commitment to do the hard work, again and again, because the labor can and will yield fruit.

In *Teachers as Cultural Workers*, Freire called for a pedagogy that is armed, arguing that it is "the fighting love of those convinced of the right and the duty to fight, to denounce and to announce" (Freire, 1998, p. 42, as cited in Darder 2011). Freire's use of the word *fight* is not to be taken literally; rather, it is a willingness to forcefully advocate for students, a fierce commitment to teaching, and active engagement in the sociopolitical, and often oppressive, processes that shape educational institutions. Radical hope is a commitment to struggle for engagement, resistance, and liberation even in the face of despair (Ryoo et al., 2009). It is a moral obligation to be visionary and idealistic (Kirylo, 2017). Leaders who practice radical care understand that radical hope is essential to their work of dismantling "contested space[s] waiting to be transformed" (Liou et al., 2016, p. 6).

WHAT RADICAL HOPE IS NOT

There are very clear distinctions that must be made between radical hope and a version of hope that is masquerading as limiting care. One example of this is the organization Teach for America (TFA), founded by Wendy Kopp in 1989, whose website describes their efforts as working

toward the day when every child will receive an excellent and equitable education. We find and nurture leaders who commit to expanding opportunity
for low-income students, beginning with at least two years teaching in a
public school. (Teach for America, n.d.)

TFA's theory of change involves developing future leaders who, after
their 2-year teaching commitment, will go on to be systems change leaders. According to TFA, 63% of their alumni stay in the field of education,
while others go on to work in other industries (Teach for America, n.d.).
    While TFA uses terms like "equitable" and "opportunity," critiques
have been leveled at the organization because its model fails to address
systemic inequities and institutional oppression that limit opportunities
for students they serve (Darling-Hammond, 2010; Darling-Hammond et
al., 2018). Their alternative certification model includes a highly truncat-
ed training process before TFA corps members are placed in classrooms
with students who would most benefit from highly skilled and fully certified teachers (Socol & Metz, 2017). As a result, students who have had
the least access to high-quality educational experiences are the figurative
guinea pigs on which TFA educators are invited to experiment. Further,
TFA and other programs like it, require relatively short-term commit-
ments to teach in underserved schools, likely contributing to teacher
turnover, which further destabilizes the same schools. Rather than making a lasting impact that disrupts deep structural oppression by ensuring
that students of color in urban schools consistently have access to fully
certified and highly trained educators, programs like TFA create temporary solutions that fail to fundamentally transform education for Black
and Latinx students and other students of color. As Anyon (2014) argues
in *Radical Possibilities*, the fundamental conditions that lead to structural
oppression in all aspects of society have to be dismantled if education for
students of color is going to improve. The TFA model, and others like it,
are masquerading as radical hope, but as they lack a sustained and honest
critique of historical and institutional inequities (Trujillo et al., 2017),
they are simply manifestations of limiting care.

RADICAL HOPE IN ACTION

Bronx principal Byron Johnson's struggle for equity was energized and
renewed by an urgent and emphatic sense of possibility, or radical hope.
His propensity for asking reflective questions led him to explore and hope.
He frequently asked, "what if . . . ?" in his talks with staff, his social media

interactions, and in conversations with me. This led Johnson to regularly make ambitious statements about his vision of education, for example stating, "I believe we can use education to change the world. I believe we can end poverty, wars, and hate in our lifetime." While this may seem like naive idealism, he made these kinds of statements frequently and without a hint of wryness or disbelief. Johnson embraced a spirit of radical hope as described by Díaz (2016) that guarded against the "despair of hopelessness" (Duncan-Andrade, 2009, p. 185).

Having a firm vision in "what could be" drove Johnson to believe that anything was possible; rather than seeing constraints, he was solution-oriented. Where a void existed, Johnson fervently believed that there was a fix waiting to be created if only one dared to dream it possible. He reminded his staff of this frequently, pushing them to see themselves as "design-thinkers." In one of his weekly "Johnson Bulletins" to the staff, he reminded them,

> As we are all realizing, teachers (all staff) have to be creators as well. We cannot just follow a textbook created by some company that doesn't know us, the community we serve, or our kids. We must use resources from a variety of sources to design authentic, rigorous, and rich learning experiences for our students. Using each other as resources, and all of the resources we have in house, in cyber space, and our PLNs (Professional Learning Networks) that we are developing with educators all over the world (Twitter) we will create the curriculum our kids need for lifelong success. (April 14, 2014)

Here, Johnson not only encouraged his teachers to be imaginative in their planning, but also reminded them they had to design instructional experiences that were responsive to the community they served. Still, a persistent challenge for Johnson was recognizing that others did not always share his sense of urgency, not knowing when to push and when to let it go.

Knowing the students and designing the school so that it met their needs was critical in his leadership practice and embodied a spirit of radical hope that spurred Johnson's leadership actions. An example of this was in his implementation of the "Genius Hour" within the students' weekly schedules. Johnson firmly believed that it was the school's responsibility to create opportunities for students rather than limit them. His unrestrained optimism of what *could* be spurred him to move from idea to reality. Despite the hesitation from some skeptical staff members, SFSJ eventually did radically alter their schedule, creating two 60-minute

"Genius Hour" blocks per week for students to pursue "passion projects" under the guidance of teachers. Not only was this a countercultural shift for a traditional school, it was absolutely unheard of for an urban middle school facing state testing to devote time to topics not covered on the test. Johnson leveraged his power to act on a vision that was fueled by radical hope. His energy and commitment to transformation inspired his teachers despite their initial skepticism. Moreover, because he had cultivated authentic relationships with his staff, the students, and their families, they trusted him enough to follow his vision.

CONCLUSION

At the onset of writing this chapter, I will admit that I was finding it hard to embrace a spirit of radical hope. The evening before, I had attended yet another contentious Board of Education meeting in New Rochelle, where community members of color, including myself, were once again speaking out about the incoming White superintendent whose reverse discrimination lawsuit in New York City felt like a slap in the face. In my remarks during the meeting, I encouraged the board members to have the moral courage to undo their mistake. I, along with other community members, had been hopeful that we might persist in our struggle for humanity; instead, I left the meeting deflated and disillusioned. I felt hopeless. And then I was reminded by conversations with others engaged in this fight that radical hope is not just about our work in this moment. It is a reminder that our work is generational—that we are points on a continuum that stretch long before we arrived and will continue long after we are gone. I was reminded of a speech given by Frederick Douglass (1867), where he said,

> The whole history of the progress of human liberty shows that all concessions yet made to her august claims, have been born of earnest struggle. . . . If there is no struggle there is no progress. . . . The struggle may be a moral one or it may be a physical one, or it may be both moral and physical, but it must be a struggle. Power concedes nothing without a demand. It never has and it never will. Find out just what a people will submit to, and you have found out the exact amount of injustice and wrong which will be imposed upon them; and these will continue till they are resisted with either words or blows, or with both. The limits of tyrants are prescribed by the endurance of those whom they oppress. (para. 1–3)

Douglass's words remind us that there is no gain without struggle. Justice is not easily won. Far from seeking to discourage, Douglass's speech puts the struggle within a broader historical and sociological context. These are hard times. And leading in schools in underresourced communities can be exhausting. This is where radical hope is essential.

The hard truth about radical hope is that it is difficult to muster and maintain. I have not yet met one leader who has not felt disillusioned or felt compelled or tempted to simply quit and move into work that didn't take such a huge emotional toll. Still, leaders who embrace a spirit of radical hope draw sustenance from the knowledge that they are part of a legacy of struggle. To quote Coretta Scott King (1969/1993), "Freedom is never really won—you earn it and win it in every generation." This sentiment was echoed in a keynote by Bishop William J. Barber II (2020) delivered at an event sponsored by the Congressional Black Caucus: "Every seat you hold is covered in blood." Bishop Barber wanted to remind us that we were only sitting in this space, holding power and privilege, as a result of prior struggles for racial liberation and justice. He went on to recall that when the Dred Scott decision was rendered, Frederick Douglass told a crowd of abolitionists that they should look upon the moment cheerfully. Each setback, Barber explained, is another catalyst ensuring that liberation can be achieved. The oppressive structures that have been so damaging to Black and Latinx communities while maintaining the status quo are not easily toppled. The overwhelming resistance that arises in response to leaders practicing radical care means that they are touching a nerve, getting closer to a tight core that is fiercely protected. Radical hope is what compels these leaders to persist.

CHAPTER 6

Conclusion

The framework of radical care in leadership that I've laid out in the preceding chapters is a call to action, an aspirational model for leadership for social justice in urban schools. To be clear, radical care is best imagined as the five individual components working synergistically. Again, radical caring in leadership involves:

- Adopting an antiracist stance
- Cultivating authentic relationships
- Believing in students' and teachers' capacity for excellence
- Leveraging power strategically
- Embracing a spirit of radical hope

These components should be viewed as fundamentally interconnected, with antiracism at their core.

Leaders who adopt an antiracist stance are unapologetically committing to understanding the role that racism has played in maintaining oppressive systems within educational systems and beyond and dismantling them. Their work, then, is centered on examining the impact of racism within their personal lives as well as within the schools they lead. Their antiracist lens allows them to critically examine the institutional policies and systems that maintain oppression for Black and Latinx students and communities. Most importantly, they engage their teachers and broader school community in engaging in antiracist work. As a result of adopting an antiracist stance, leaders who practice radical care are attuned to critically examine school practices and systems, and they actively work to disrupt institutional oppression in all forms.

This antiracism stance informs all aspects of the work of leaders practicing radical care, including working to cultivate authentic relationships with their students and families, as well as the educators in the school. As antiracist practitioners, they are mindful of engaging their communities from an asset-based approach, and they seek to understand the historical and institutional oppression that has impacted those communities.

These relationships, which are grounded in mutual trust, allow the leader to leverage them to demand excellence from the students and teachers. Here, too, radical care's antiracist component is activated because rather than embracing a deficit perspective that limits possibilities for students and teachers, leaders who practice radical care demand excellence because they fervently believe that it is possible to achieve. This is not a matter of leaders having high standards to satisfy a mandate; rather, it is a function of a leader practicing radical care who understands that, when the barriers that limit their students' and teachers' capacity to exceed their potential are dismantled, excellence is infinitely possible.

Leaders who practice radical care also leverage their power to enact critical changes within their schools, and to advocate for broader systemic reforms, all in the interest of dismantling barriers that are the byproducts of systemic oppression. The drive for transformation is informed by an antiracist mindset and a moral imperative to leverage power for good. It is also informed by a spirit of radical hope that urgently imagines and agitates for more just and equitable possibilities for Black and Latinx children in schools.

THE COMPONENTS OF RADICAL CARE WORKING SYNERGISTICALLY

To illustrate the interconnected nature of the components of radical care, I return to an earlier example from Chapter 4 when Bronx middle school principal Byron Johnson leveraged his power to work to advocate for parents' rights to opt their children out of standardized exams. As I described in that chapter, Johnson fervently believed that rather than improving the educational experiences and outcomes of students of color, standardized testing was shrinking the curriculum and stifling Black and Latinx students' opportunities for academically rigorous learning. First, Johnson worked within his school to encourage curricular and instructional innovation among his staff and discouraged them from teaching to the test. He also began meeting with parents within his school community to discuss the impact of high-stakes tests, and later began a more public rejection of the standardized tests because of their impact on Black and Latinx children.

Johnson strategically leveraged his power to advocate on behalf of students because, as a leader who practiced radical care, he also had a critical understanding of how the exams were a function of systemic oppression. Moreover, as a leader adopting an antiracist stance, Johnson's critique of the exams extended to how they also constrained resource allocation to urban schools serving primarily Black and Latinx children. Rather than have opportunities to engage in design thinking and exploration, adherence to high-stakes accountability policies tended to limit those choices. Johnson rejected this through his public resistance but also leveraged his power to reimagine how the schedule could be changed to better tap into students' inner genius and pursuit of their interests, while also encouraging teachers' innovation in their teaching practices. His cultivation of authentic relationships throughout the school community enabled these changes because the adults and the children trusted that they could safely take risks and learn from the challenges. Johnson's insistence that the students and teachers had the capacity for excellence strengthened and solidified their trust in him and in one another. Furthermore, Johnson's embrace of a spirit of radical hope motivated him and others around him to firmly believe that the dismantling of an oppressive accountability structure through resistance and transformation was possible.

Johnson's engagement in the opt-out efforts and his critique of high-stakes testing policies illustrate the interdependence of the five components of radical care and also demonstrate the powerful impact this kind of leadership has on students and their families, as well as educators. Rather than adopting a "drill and kill" approach to the tests, he opted for curricular innovation. Johnson's explicit articulation of how the testing policies reinforced structural oppression for Black and Latinx children encouraged students in his school to activate their agency in their learning and to develop their own critical analysis of systems and oppression. Likewise, teachers were also engaged in a critical analysis of institutions and understanding how transformation was possible through conscious curricular choices that rejected dominant frameworks. Similarly, through his engagement of community members, Johnson rejected pressure from the Department of Education to not inform parents of their rights regarding the tests. Far from encouraging parents to opt their children out, he affirmed their agency in making decisions in their children's best interest.

This is just one illustration but it underscores how the five components of radical care are highly integrated. A similar exercise can be undertaken with other examples throughout the book and underscores the need to explicitly examine effective urban school leadership practices through a radical care framework. And yet what is also striking about the leaders highlighted throughout the book is that they rarely, if ever, credited their leadership practices to institutions of higher education. Rather, these leaders often talked about their families or school experiences in their formative years as informing what they say is a moral calling. While this is intriguing, as I write this chapter in the first week of January 2021, after a year of a so-called "racial reckoning" and a recent insurrection on the United States's Capitol Hill, I am more convinced than ever that we must do more in educator preparation programs to explicitly teach radical care for aspiring school leaders, and teachers, too, if we are truly going to transform education.

RADICAL CARE IN INSTITUTIONS OF HIGHER EDUCATION

We frequently make assumptions that institutions of higher education (IHEs), and schools of education, in particular, are enlightened spaces where this transformative work is already underway. This is a deeply flawed and dangerous assumption. The truth is that many professors, especially within schools of education, were once teachers and leaders who (un)consciously reproduced the inequities that I have described, enacting limiting, not radical, care. IHEs are not immune and, in fact, are too often complicit in reinforcing systemic oppression in their teaching (Genao, 2020; McClellan, 2010) and their research (Patel, 2016). The cycle remains unbroken if we assume that professors are, themselves, enacting radical care. Whereas school reform is often situated or framed as a K–12 issue, in fact, paradigm shifts must occur within programs preparing teachers, school counselors, social workers, and psychologists, as well as leadership preparation programs. In order for those to shift, however, professors of education and related educational fields must also undergo their own transformation.

In New York State, the recently adopted Culturally Responsive/ Sustaining Education (New York State Education Department, 2019) outlines various stakeholder groups that are impacted by the new initiative, including IHEs and teacher education programs. This work must begin with transforming the mindsets and paradigms of those who are working with people who are training to work with kids in schools. Ongoing learning around the five components of radical care is essential for higher education faculty who are responsible for training classroom educators and mental health professionals, who later become school principals and assistant principals. We cannot expect higher education faculty to train future educators to engage in antiracist pedagogical practices if they themselves are unable to emulate and engage in those practices.

Hand in hand with ongoing learning for college faculty is a shift in how IHEs prioritize certain activities when awarding tenure and promotion.

Rather than an overemphasis on scholarship that is disconnected from the practical work of developing school professionals who are committed to radical care, and inaccessible (figuratively and literally) to practitioners, college faculty should be rewarded for the transformational impact we have on our students and the communities they are learning to serve. This begins with developing faculty to be antiracist practitioners and researchers. Similar to the school leaders' work, radical care in IHEs require that we examine our own deeply held beliefs and how those beliefs serve to reinforce institutional oppression through our teaching and research. We, too, need to write our racial autobiographies to examine our racial histories and literacy. We must also engage in community equity audits (Green, 2016) to understand the communities in which our IHEs are situated and to critically examine how our colleges and universities reinforce or work to dismantle institutional oppression.

Faculty in IHEs can work alongside those we are training to cultivate authentic relationships with partner pre-K–12 schools, which also deepens our relationships with those we teach. We must see the assets in communities as building blocks to create the foundation for building relationships. Too often, educators who go into the profession have a savior mindset. A deficit lens is almost unavoidable for people coming out of these programs. Consciously engaging Yosso's (2005) theory of community cultural wealth, we can begin to undercut this inevitability and build a growing field of educators who understand that community and schooling go hand in hand, and that communities are imbued with knowledge, capital, and wealth.

The relationships we develop with aspiring leaders and educators should be leveraged to push for excellence in our students. Just as we push them to examine and disrupt deficit thinking and limiting care, faculty must also engage in that work. Faculty are not immune to limited beliefs about our students. We have work to do! Again, this is about examining our deeply held mental models that are manifested in the ways we do the work, even when the rhetoric we espouse is different. Our students will rise to the level of our expectations if we expect excellence from them and provide them with the supports to fulfill their potential. I have had a number of students, primarily students of color, who have entered the educational leadership program, pursuing their second, or sometimes third, graduate degree, whose written work was largely below professional standards. This was never because the student lacked the intellect or the potential to be a successful leader. Rather, they had never been explicitly told that their writing needed improvement, nor had they been given the tools or support to improve. These educators typically worked in Bronx schools, and because they lacked some of these critical writing skills, they were unintentionally failing to prepare their Black and Latinx students to become skilled writers.

Faculty in IHEs must strategically leverage our power to create the conditions that are necessary for radical care to take root. We must forcefully and publicly advance an agenda that is concerned with the equal access to rigorous, high-quality educational opportunities for our students and for the students they serve. Equally important, faculty must use our power and privilege within the academy to stand alongside pre-K–12 educators and leaders who are resisting policies that reproduce inequality. This might take shape in different ways. For example, faculty members might participate in protests and rallies alongside school leaders and educators to demonstrate our solidarity. Our institutional affiliations can provide them with much-needed protection as they work to resist policies that are harmful to the communities they serve. We must also be intentionally and explicitly in conversation with those in the field so that we might learn from them what they need from us. There is urgency in this work, and if we also embrace a spirit of radical hope, we can act with purpose and faith in what could be.

CLOSING THOUGHTS:
LEVERAGING PRIVILEGE TO ENACT RADICAL CARE

I want to close with a reminder that if you are reading this book, you already possess a tremendous amount of privilege. And too often, those of us with privilege are complicit in the reproduction of systemic oppression either because we are silent or numbed to a point of inaction. But with privilege comes a tremendous responsibility and opportunity to use our power, our positions, and our access to disrupt inequity and to work to create the schools that our brilliant Black and Latinx kids deserve. So I urge all of us to use our privilege and lead with radical care.

School Descriptions

Bridges Institute

Bridges Institute is a small urban high school founded in 1994 as part of the restructuring of a failing NYC comprehensive high school. Located in one of the poorest congressional districts in the country, Bridges is a zoned high school, open to the predominantly Black and Latinx students from the local community. Originally staffed by a small group of veteran educators who had previously worked with Deborah Meier in the legendary Central Park East Secondary School in Manhattan, the school's founders were dedicated to interrupting the educational neglect of their students through carefully designed student-centered instruction and authentic assessment, as well as through active engagement in relevant social issues. Committed to providing a high-quality education to historically marginalized youth, Bridges continues to aim to prepare students for college. The staff capitalizes on the small size of roughly 450 students to create meaningful relationships with their students, and the word "family" is often used to describe the school community.

Innovation High School

Founded in 2003, Innovation High School is a zoned high school, open to the predominantly Latinx and Black students from the local community. Serving roughly 340 students, Innovation is co-located with five other high schools on the campus of a former large comprehensive high school. Nearly 90% of the students qualify for free or reduced-price lunch. In 2014 the school was allowed to join the New York Performance Standards Consortium and transitioned from a Regents-based assessment system to a portfolio-based assessment tasks system of assessment, prioritizing inquiry and depth. Innovation High School is a college-preparatory school with an emphasis on developing students' critical thinking skills.

Every student is assigned to an advisor, and students remain with their advisor throughout their high school career.

School for Social Justice

Founded in 2009, the School for Social Justice (SFSJ) is located in an educational campus in the northeast section of the Bronx. The building that houses SFSJ also hosts an elementary school and a districtwide school designated for students with severe cognitive and/or emotional disabilities. Not too far from a busy highway, this public middle school is surrounded on one side by numerous auto body and mechanical repair shops and on the other by private single- and multiple-family homes and a public housing development, where many of the school's students reside. SFSJ serves children in grades 6–8 and is designated as a zoned school with open admissions. Unlike many other Bronx schools where Latinx students are in the majority, at the time of this study SFSJ's student body comprised 62% Black, 34% Latinx, and 3% White, with 82% of the roughly 250 student population qualifying for free or reduced-price lunch.

Notes

Introduction

1. All names of schools and school personnel are pseudonyms.
2. Junot Díaz's history of abuse toward women is reprehensible. I cite him here with a great deal of hesitation solely because his essay introduced me to the concept of radical hope that I draw on for my framework of radical care.

Chapter 1

1. The Four Is of oppression and advantage is a framework commonly used by grassroots and equity-focused organizations, but the author of the original framework is unknown.

Chapter 2

1. While these relationships were important, absent an analysis of the broader structural inequities and systemic racism impacting my students and the broader community, I unconsciously lowered my expectations for my students and myself, and practiced a form of limiting care (see Introduction). I highlight this here to underscore the complexity of leading with radical care.

References

Amrein, A. L., & Berliner, D. C. (2003). The effects of high-stakes testing on student motivation and learning. *Educational Leadership, 60*(5), 32–33.

Amrein, A. L., & Berliner, D. C. (2008). High-stakes testing, uncertainty, and student learning. *Education Policy Analysis Archives, 10*(18), 1–74.

Antrop-González, R. (2011). *Schools as radical sanctuaries: Decolonizing urban education through the eyes of youth of color.* Information Age Publishing.

Antrop-González, R., & De Jesús, A. (2006). Toward a theory of critical care in urban small school reform: Examining structures and pedagogies of caring in two Latino community-based schools. *International Journal of Qualitative Studies in Education, 19*(4), 409–433.

Anyon, J. (1980). Social class and the hidden curriculum of work. *Journal of Education, 162*(1), 67–92.

Anyon, J. (2014). *Radical possibilities: Public policy, urban education, and a new social movement* (2nd ed.). Routledge.

Anzaldúa, G. (2012). *Borderlands / La frontera: The new mestiza* (4th ed.). Aunt Lute Books.

Au, W. (2008). *Unequal by design: High-stakes testing and the standardization of inequity*. Routledge.

Au, W. (2011). Teaching under the new Taylorism: High-stakes testing and the standardization of the 21st century curriculum. *Journal of Curriculum Studies, 43*(1), 25–45. https://doi.org/10.1080/00220272.2010.521261

Au, W. (2016). Meritocracy 2.0: High-stakes, standardized testing as a racial project of neoliberal multiculturalism. *Educational Policy, 30*(1), 39–62. https://doi.org/10.1177/0895904815614916

Baker, R. (2012). The effects of high-stakes testing on arts education. *Arts Education Policy Review, 113*(1), 17–25.

Barber, W. J., II. (2020, February 4). *Keynote* address. Congressional Black Caucus: 2020 National Black Leadership Summit: An Emergency Convening, Washington, DC. https://cbc.house.gov/2020summit/

Bass, L. (2012). When care trumps justice: The operationalization of Black feminist caring in educational leadership. *International Journal of Qualitative Studies in Education, 25*(1), 73–87. https://doi.org/10.1080/09518398.2011.647721

Bass, L. (Ed.). (2016). *Black mask-ulinity: A framework for black masculine caring.* Peter Lang.

Beauboeuf-Lafontant, T. (2002). A womanist experience of caring: Understanding the pedagogy of exemplary Black women teachers. *The Urban Review, 34*(1), 71–86.

Bell, D. A. (1992). *Faces at the bottom of the well: The permanence of racism* (Reprint ed.). Basic Books.

Billings, D. (2016). *Deep denial: The persistence of white supremacy in the United States history and life.* Crandall, Dostie, & Douglass Books.

Bloom, H. S., Thompson, S. L., & Unterman, R. (2010). *Transforming the high school experience: How New York City's new small schools are boosting student achievement and graduation rates.* MDRC.

Bogotch, I. E. (2002). Educational leadership and social justice: Practice into theory. *Journal of School Leadership, 12*(2), 138–156.

Bonilla-Silva, E. (2017). *Racism without racists: Color-blind racism and the persistence of racial inequality in America* (5th ed.). Rowman & Littlefield.

Bromberg, M., & Theokas, C. (2013). *Breaking the glass ceiling of achievement for low-income students and students of color.* The Education Trust. Available at https://edtrust.org/resource/breaking-the-glass-ceiling-of-achievement-for-low-income-students-and-students-of-color/

Burns, D., Darling-Hammond, L., & Scott, C. (2019, September). *Closing the opportunity gap: How positive outlier districts in California are pursuing equitable access to deeper learning.* Learning Policy Institute. https://learningpolicyinstitute.org/product/positive-outliers-closing-opportunity-gap-report

Cardichon, J., Darling-Hammond, L., Yang, M., Scott, C., Shields, P. M., & Burns, D. (2020). *Inequitable opportunity to learn: Student access to certified and experienced teachers.* Learning Policy Institute.

Curry, M. W. (2016). Will you stand for me? Authentic cariño and transformative rites of passage in an urban high school. *American Educational Research Journal, 53*(4), 883–918.

Dantley, M. E. (2009). African American educational leadership: Critical, purposive, and spiritual. In L. Foster & L. C. Tillman (Eds.), *African American perspectives on leadership in schools: Building a culture of empowerment* (pp. 39–52). Rowman & Littlefield.

Darder, A. (2011). Teaching as an act of love: Reflections on Paulo Freire and his contributions to our lives and our work. *Counterpoints, 418,* 179–194. https://www.jstor.org/stable/42981647

Darling-Hammond, L. (2010). *The flat world and education: How America's commitment to equity will determine our future.* Teachers College Press.

Darling-Hammond, L., Sutcher, L., & Carver-Thomas, D. (2018). *Teacher shortages in California: Status, sources, and potential solutions* [Research Brief]. Learning Policy Institute.

Delgado, R., & Stefancic, J. (2017). *Critical race theory: An introduction* (3rd ed.). NYU Press.

deMause, N. (2016, March 28). Low-income parents are caught between the growing opt-out movement and the city's attempts to clamp down on dissent. *Village Voice.* http://www.villagevoice.com/news/low-income-parents-are-caught-between-the-growing-opt-out-movement-and-the-city-s-attempts-to-clamp-down-on-dissent-8447023

DiAngelo, R. (2018). *White fragility: Why it's so hard for White people to talk about racism* (reprint ed.). Beacon Press.

Díaz, J. (2016, November 21). Under President Trump, radical hope is our best weapon. *The New Yorker.* https://www.newyorker.com/

magazine/2016/11/21/under-president-trump-radical-hope-is-our-best-weapon

Douglass, F. (1867, August 4). *Frederick Douglass declares there is "No progress without struggle.* SHEC: Resources for Teachers. https://herb.ashp.cuny.edu/items/show/1245

Duckworth, A. (2018). *Grit: The power of passion and perseverance.* Scribner.

Duncan-Andrade, J. (2009). Note to educators: Hope required when growing roses in concrete. *Harvard Educational Review, 79*(2), 181–194.

Dweck, C. S. (2016). *Mindset: The new psychology of success.* Ballantine Books.

Education Secretary Confirmation Hearing, U.S. Senate Education Committee, 117th Cong. (2021). https://www.c-span.org/video/?508484-1/education-secretary-nominee-miguel-cardona-testifies-confirmation-hearing&live

Fine, M. (2005). Not in our name: Reclaiming the democratic vision of small school reform. *Rethinking Schools, 19*(4), 11–14.

Foster, L., & Tillman, L. C. (2009). Introduction. In L. Foster & L. C. Tillman (Eds.), *African American perspectives on leadership in schools: Building a culture of empowerment* (pp. 1–13). Rowman & Littlefield.

Foster, M. (1998). *Black teachers on teaching.* The New Press.

Genao, S. (2020). (Re)building New York City's communities: Meeting the needs for bi/multilingual educational leadership preparation. In S. Genao & N. M. Gray-Nicolas (Eds.), *(Re)building bi/multilingual leaders for socially just communities.* (pp. 1–17). Information Age Publishing.

Ginwright, S. (2016). *Hope and healing in urban education: How urban activists and teachers are reclaiming matters of the heart.* Routledge.

Gooden, M. A.. (2020, October 13). What an anti-racist principal must do. *Education Week.* https://www.edweek.org/leadership/opinion-what-an-anti-racist-principal-must-do/2020/10

Gooden, M. A., & Dantley, M. E. (2012). Centering race in a framework for leadership preparation. *Journal of Research on Leadership Education, 7*(2), 237–253.

Goodman, S. (2018). *It's not about grit: Trauma, inequity, and the power of transformative teaching.* Teachers College Press.

Gottlieb, D., & Schneider, J. (2020). Educational accountability is out of step—now more than ever. *Phi Delta Kappan, 102*(1), 24–25. https://doi.org/10.1177/0031721720956842

Graham, G., Parker, S., Wilkins, J., Fraser, R., Westfall, S., & Tembo, M. (2013). The effects of high-stakes testing on elementary art, music, and physical education. *Journal of Physical Education, Recreation, and Dance, 73*(8), 51–54.

Green, T. L. (2016). Community-based equity audits: A practical approach for educational leaders to support equitable community-school improvements. *Educational Administration Quarterly, 53*(1), 3–39.

Hagopian, J., & Jones, D. (Eds.). (2020). *Black lives matter at school.* Haymarket Books.

Hanlon, B. (2009). A typology of inner-ring suburbs: Class, race, and ethnicity in U.S. suburbia. *City & Community, 8*(3), 221–246. https://doi.org/10.1111/j.1540-6040.2009.01287.x

Hannah-Jones, N. (2016, June 9). Choosing a school for my daughter in a segregated city. *The New York Times*. https://www.nytimes.com/2016/06/12/magazine/choosing-a-school-for-my-daughter-in-a-segregated-city.html

Hantzopoulos, M. (2016). *Restoring dignity in public schools: Human rights education in action*. Teachers College Press.

Hantzopoulos, M., Rivera-McCutchen, R. L., & Tyner-Mullings, A. R. (2021). Reframing school culture through project-based assessment tasks: Cultivating transformative agency and humanizing practices in NYC public schools. *Teachers College Record, 123*(4), n.p.

Hantzopoulos, M., & Tyner-Mullings, A. R. (2012). Preface. In M. Hantzopoulos & A. R. Tyner-Mullings (Eds.), *Critical small schools: Beyond privatization in New York City urban educational reform* (pp. xix–xxiv). Information Age.

Harris, C. I. (1993). Whiteness as property. *Harvard Law Review, 106*(8), 1707–1791. https://doi.org/10.2307/1341787

Hilliard, A., III. (1991). Do we have the will to educate all children? *Educational Leadership, 49*(1), 31–36.

Hip Hop Saves Lives. (2014, October 7). *We Will Not Be Silent || KHK CASA Middle school* [Video]. YouTube. https://www.youtube.com/watch?v=q7D-5mTXyL6o

Horsford, S. D. (2010). Mixed feelings about mixed schools: Superintendents on the complex legacy of school desegregation. *Educational Administration Quarterly, 46*(3), 287–321.

Horsford, S. D. (2011). *Learning in a burning house: Educational inequality, ideology, and (dis)integration*. Teachers College Press.

Irvine, J. J. (1991). *Black students and school failure: Policies, practices, and prescriptions*. Praeger.

Irvine, J. J. (2003). *Educating teachers for diversity: Seeing with a cultural eye*. Teachers College Press.

Ishimaru, A. M. (2020). *Just schools: Building equitable collaborations with families and communities*. Teachers College Press.

Jackson, I., Sealey-Ruiz, Y., & Watson, W. (2014). Reciprocal love: Mentoring Black and Latino males through an ethos of care. *Urban Education, 49*, 394–417. https://doi.org/10.1177/0042085913519336

Jean-Marie, G., Normore, A. H., & Brooks, J. S. (2009). Leadership for social justice: Preparing 21st century school leaders for a new social order. *Journal of Research on Leadership Education, 4*(1), 1–31.

Kamenetz, A. (2015). *The test: Why our schools are obsessed with standardized testing but you don't have to be*. PublicAffairs.

Kelley, R.D.G. (2002). *Freedom dreams: The Black radical imagination*. Beacon Press.

Kendi, I. X. (2017). *Stamped from the beginning: The definitive history of racist ideas in America* (Reprint ed.). Bold Type Books.

Khalifa, M. A. (2012). A *re-new-ed* paradigm in successful urban school leadership: Principal as community leader. *Educational Administration Quarterly, 48*(3), 424–467. https://doi.org/10.1177/0013161X11432922

King, C. S. (1993). *My life with Martin Luther King Jr.* (revised ed.). Henry Holt. (Original published 1969)

King, J. E. (1991). Dysconscious racism: Ideology, identity, and the miseducation of teachers. *The Journal of Negro Education, 60*(2), 133–146. https://doi.org/10.2307/2295605

Kirylo, J. D. (2017). Hate won, but love will have the final word: Critical pedagogy, liberation theology, and the moral imperative of resistance. *Policy Futures in Education, 15*(5), 590–601. https://doi.org/10.1177/1478210317707454

Kohli, R. (2018). Behind school doors: The impact of hostile racial climates on urban teachers of color. *Urban Education, 53*(3), 307–333. https://doi.org/10.1177/0042085916636653

Kolodner, M. (2015, September 29). Once sold as the solution, small high schools are now on the back burner. *The Hechinger Report.* http://hechingerreport.org/once-sold-as-the-solution-small-high-schools-are-now-on-the-back-burner/

Kozol, J. (1991). *Savage inequalities: Children in America's schools.* Harper Perennial.

Kozol, J. (2005). *The shame of the nation: The restoration of apartheid schooling in America.* Crown.

Kuscera, J., & Orfield, G. (2014). *New York State's extreme school segregation: Inequality, inaction and a damaged future.* The Civil Rights Project/ProyectoDerechosCiviles.https://civilrightsproject.ucla.edu/research/k-12-education/integration-and-diversity/ny-norflet-report-placeholder/Kucsera-New-York-Extreme-Segregation-2014.pdf

Ladson-Billings, G. (1998). Just what is critical race theory and what's it doing in a nice field like education? *International Journal of Qualitative Studies in Education, 11*(1), 7–24. https://doi.org/10.1080/095183998236863

Ladson-Billings, G. (2006). From the achievement gap to the education debt: Understanding achievement in U.S. schools. *Educational Researcher, 35*(7), 3–12. https://doi.org/10.3102/0013189X035007003

Ladson-Billings, G., & Tate, W.F.I. (1995). Toward a critical race theory of education. *Teachers College Record, 97*(1), 47–68.

Lanas, M., & Zembylas, M. (2015). Towards a transformational political concept of love in critical education. *Studies in Philosophy and Education, 34*(1), 31–44. https://doi.org/10.1007/s11217-014-9424-5

Lewis-McCoy, R. L. (2014). *Inequality in the promised land: Race, resources, and suburban schooling.* Stanford University Press.

Liou, D. D., Marsh, T.E.J., & Antrop-González, R. (2016). The spatiality of schooling: A quest for equitable classrooms and high expectations for low-income students of color. *InterActions: UCLA Journal of Education and Information Studies, 12*(2), 1–20.

Lomotey, K. (1993). African-American principals: Bureaucrat/administrators and ethno-humanists. *Urban Education, 27*(4), 395–412. https://doi.org/10.1177/0042085993027004005

López, G. R. (2003). The (racially neutral) politics of education: A critical race theory perspective. *Educational Administration Quarterly, 39*(1), 68–94. https://doi.org/10.1177/0013161X02239761

Louis, K. S., Murphy, J., & Smylie, M. (2016). Caring leadership in schools: Findings from exploratory analysis. *Educational Administration Quarterly, 52*(2), 310–348.

Love, B. L. (2019). *We want to do more than survive: Abolitionist teaching and the pursuit of educational freedom*. Beacon Press.

Love, B. L. (2020, June 23). *Abolitionist teaching and the future of our schools* [Panel/Video]. Haymarket Books. https://www.haymarketbooks.org/blogs/179-abolitionist-teaching-and-the-future-of-our-schools

Luna, R. (2013). *Stolen Education* [Documentary]. Alemán/Luna Productions. https://www.amazon.com/Stolen-Education-Enrique-Aleman/dp/B079395S6X

Marshall, C., Patterson, J. A., & Rogers, D. L. (1996). Caring as career: An alternative perspective for educational administration. *Educational Administration Quarterly*, *32*, 271–294. https://doi.org/10.1177/0013161X96032002005

Martinez, M. A., & Rivera-McCutchen, R. L. (in press). The collective and unique contributions of Latina urban school leaders: Testimonios of advocacy and resistance. In N. W. Arnold, A. Onsaloo, & R. O. Guillaume (Eds.), *The handbook of urban educational leadership* (2nd ed.). Rowman & Littlefield.

McClellan, P. A. (2010). Toward critical servant leadership in graduate schools of education: From theoretical construct to social justice praxis. In S. D. Horsford (Ed.), *New perspectives in educational leadership: Exploring social, political, and community contexts and meaning* (pp. 89–108). Peter Lang.

McClellan, P. A. (2020). Portraits of Black girls: Reflections on schooling and leadership of a Black woman principal in the age of adultism. *Journal of Educational Administration and History*, *52*(3), 256–269. https://doi.org/10.1080/00220620.2020.1786357

McNeil, L. M., Coppola, E., Radigan, J., & Vasquez Heilig, J. (2008). Avoidable losses: High-stakes accountability and the dropout crisis. *Education Policy Analysis Archives*, *16*(3). https://dialnet.unirioja.es/servlet/articulo?codigo=3199215

Mediratta, K., & Karp, J. (2003). *Parent power and urban school reform: The story of mothers on the move*. New York University Institute for Education and Social Policy.

Meier, D. (2003). *In schools we trust: Creating communities of learning in an era of testing and standardization*. Beacon Press.

Miller, P. M., Brown, T., & Hopson, R. (2011). Centering love, hope, and trust in the community: Transformative urban leadership informed by Paulo Freire. *Urban Education*, *46*(5), 1078–1099. https://doi.org/10.1177/0042085910395951

New York Performance Standards Consortium (n.d.). New York Performance Standards Consortium. http://www.performanceassessment.org/

New York State Education Department. (2019). *Culturally responsive-sustaining education framework*.

Noddings, N. (2005). *The challenge to care in schools: An alternative approach to education* (2nd ed.). Teachers College Press.

Noguera, P., Darling-Hammond, L., & Friedlaender, D. (2015). *Equal opportunity for deeper learning*. Jobs for the Future.

NYC Department of Education. (2015). *New York City community schools strategic plan*. https://www1.nyc.gov/assets/communityschools/downloads/

pdf/community-schools-strategic-plan.pdf

Patel, L. (2016). *Decolonizing educational research: From ownership to answerability*. Routledge.

Payne, C. M. (2008). *So much reform, so little change: The persistence of failure in urban schools*. Harvard Education Press.

Picower, B. (2012). *Practice what you teach: Social justice education in the classroom and the streets*. Routledge.

Picower, B. (2021). *Reading, writing, and racism: Disrupting whiteness in teacher education and in the classroom*. Beacon Press.

Price, P. G. (2009). African-centered pedagogy and womanist caring: Reclaiming Black children for success. In L. Foster & L. C. Tillman (Eds.), *African American perspectives on leadership in schools: Building a culture of empowerment* (pp. 57–71). Rowman & Littlefield.

Radd, S. I., Generett, G. G., Gooden, M. A., & Theoharis, G. (2021). *Five practices for equity-focused leadership*. ASCD.

Ravitch, D. (2013). *Reign of error: The hoax of the privatization movement and the danger to America's public schools*. Alfred A. Knopf.

Rivera-McCutchen, R. L. (2012). Considering context: Exploring a small school's struggle to maintain its educational vision. In M. Hantzopoulos & A. R. Tyner-Mullings (Eds.), *Critical small schools: Moving beyond privatization in New York City public school reform* (pp. 21–39). Information Age.

Rivera-McCutchen, R. L. (2014). The moral imperative of social justice leadership: A critical component of effective practice. *The Urban Review, 46*(4), 747–763. https://doi.org/10.1007/s11256-014-0297-2

Rivera-McCutchen, R. L. (2019). Armed love in school leadership: Resisting inequality and injustice in schooling. *Leadership and Policy in Schools, 18*(2), 237–247. https://doi.org/10.1080/15700763.2019.1611867

Rivera-McCutchen, R. L. (2020). "We don't got time for grumbling": Toward an ethic of radical care in urban school leadership. *Educational Administration Quarterly, 57*(2), 257–289. https://doi.org/10.1177/0013161X20925892

Rivera-McCutchen, R. L. (2021, March 17). White privilege and power in the NYS opt out movement. *Teachers College Record*.

Rolón-Dow, R. (2005). Critical care: A color(full) analysis of care narratives in the schooling experiences of Puerto Rican girls. *American Educational Research Journal, 42*(1), 77–111. https://doi.org/10.3102/00028312042001077

Rothstein, R. (2017). *The color of law: A forgotten history of how our government segregated America*. Liveright.

Roy, A. (2020). The pandemic is a portal. *Rethinking Schools, 34*(4), 46–47.

Ryoo, J. J., Crawford, J., Moreno, D., & McLaren, P. (2009). Critical spiritual pedagogy: Reclaiming humanity through a pedagogy of integrity, community, and love. *Power and Education, 1*(1), 132–146. https://doi.org/10.2304/power.2009.1.1.132

Shedd, C. (2015). *Unequal city: Race, schools, and perceptions of injustice*. Russell Sage Foundation.

Siddle Walker, V. (1996). *Their highest potential: An African American school community in the segregated south*. University of North Carolina Press.

Siddle Walker, V. (2018). *The lost education of Horace Tate: Uncovering the hidden heroes who fought for justice in schools*. The New Press.

Siddle Walker, V., & Archung, K. N. (2003). The segretated schooling of Blacks in the southern United States and South Africa. *Comparative Education Review, 47*(1), 21–40.

Skrla, L. E., McKenzie, K. B., & Scheurich, J. J. (Eds.). (2009). *Using equity audits to create equitable and excellent schools.* Corwin.

Smith, B. (2000). Quantity matters: Annual instructional time in an urban school system. *Educational Administration Quarterly, 36*(5), 652–682. https://doi.org/10.1177/00131610021969155

Socol, A. R., & Metz, R. (2017). *Tackling gaps in access to strong teachers: Five ways state leaders can make a difference.* The Education Trust.

Solórzano, D. G., & Pérez Huber, L. (2020). *Racial microaggressions: Using critical race theory to respond to everyday racism.* Teachers College Press.

Solórzano, D. G., & Yosso, T. J. (2002). Critical race methodology: Counter-storytelling as an analytical framework for education research. *Qualitative Inquiry, 8*(1), 23–44.

Teach For America. (n.d.). Home page: What we do. https://www.teachforamerica.org/

Terbeck, F. (2020). Defining suburbs: An evaluation and comparison of four methods. *The Professional Geographer, 72*(4), 586–597 . https://doi.org/10.1080/00330124.2020.1758574

The Education Trust. (2014a). *The state of education for African American students.* The Education Trust. https://1k9gl1yevnfp2lpq1dhrqe17-wpengine.netdna-ssl.com/wp-content/uploads/2013/10/TheStateofEducation-forAfricanAmericanStudents_EdTrust_June2014.pdf

The Education Trust. (2014b). *The state of education for Latino students.* The Education Trust. https://1k9gl1yevnfp2lpq1dhrqe17-wpengine.netd-na-ssl.com/wp-content/uploads/2013/10/TheStateofEducationforLatino Students_EdTrust_June2014.pdf

Theoharis, G. (2009). *The school leaders our children deserve: Seven keys to equity, social justice, and school reform.* Teachers College Press.

Tichnor-Wagner, A., & Allen, D. (2016). Accountable for care: Cultivating caring school communities in urban high schools. *Leadership and Policy in Schools, 15*(4), 406–447.

Tillman, L. C. (2008). The scholarship of Dr. Asa G. Hilliard, III: Implications for Black principal leadership. *Review of Educational Research, 78*(3), 589–607.

Trujillo, T., Scott, J., & Rivera, M. (2017). Follow the yellow brick road: Teach For America and the making of educational leaders. *American Journal of Education, 123*(3), 353–391. https://doi.org/10.1086/691232

Tyner-Mullings, A. R. (2012). Redefining success: How CPESS students reached the goals that mattered. In M. Hantzopoulos & A. R. Tyner-Mullings (Eds.), *Critical small schools: Beyond privatization in New York City urban educational reform* (pp. 137–166). Information Age.

Tyner-Mullings, A. R. (2015). *Enter the alternative school: Critical answers to questions in urban education.* Paradigm.

University Council for Educational Administration. (n.d.) *Neighborhood walk PLE: Module 4.* http://www.ucea.org/fipse/ple-1-module-5/

U.S. Commission on Civil Rights (USCCR). (2018). *Public education funding inequity in an era of increasing concentration of poverty and resegregation*[Briefingreport].http://www.usccr.gov/pubs/2018//2018-01-10-Education-Inequity.pdf

Valenzuela, A. (1999). *Subtractive schooling: U.S.-Mexican youth and the politics of caring.* State University of New York Press.

Vasquez Heilig, J., & Darling-Hammond, L. (2008). Accountability Texas-style: The progress and learning of urban minority students in a high-stakes testing context. *Educational Evaluation and Policy Analysis, 30*(2), 75–110. https://doi.org/10.3102/0162373708317689

Volger, K. (2003). Where does social studies fit in a high-stakes testing environment? *The Social Studies, 94*(5), 207–211. https://doi.org/10.1080/00377990309600208

Warren, M. R., & Mapp, K. L. (2011). *A match on dry grass: Community organizing as a catalyst for school reform.* Oxford University Press.

Watson, T. N. (2020). Harlem's "motherwork" post-*Brown*: Implications for urban school leaders. *Journal of Educational Administration and History, 52*(3), 244–255. https://doi.org/10.1080/00220620.2020.1761779

Wildhagen, T. (2012). How teachers and schools contribute to racial differences in the realization of academic potential. *Teachers College Record, 114*(7), 1–27.

Wilkerson, I. (2020). *Caste: The origins of our discontents.* Random House.

Willis, P. (1981). *Learning to labor: How working class kids get working class jobs.* Columbia University Press.

Wilson, C. M. (2015). Refusing Detroit's public school failure: African American women's educational advocacy and critical care versus the politics of disposability. *Education Policy Analysis Archives, 23*(125), 1–33. https://doi.org/10.14507/epaa.v23.1777

Wilson, C. M. (2016). Enacting critical care and transformative leadership in schools highly impacted by poverty: An African-American principal's counter narrative. *International Journal of Leadership in Education, 19*(5), 557–577. https://doi.org/10.1080/13603124.2015.1023360

Witherspoon, N., & Arnold, B. M. (2010). Pastoral care: Notions of caring and the Black female principal. *Journal of Negro Education, 79*(3), 220–232.

Woodson, C. G. (1977). *The mis-education of the Negro* (2nd ed.). Associated Publishers. (Original published in 1933)

Yamamura, E. K., Martinez, M. A., & Saenz, V. B. (2010). Moving beyond high school expectations: Examining stakeholders' responsibility for increasing Latina/o students' college readiness. *High School Journal, 93*(3), 126–149.

Yosso, T. J. (2005). Whose culture has capital? A critical race theory discussion of community cultural wealth. *Race Ethnicity and Education, 8*(1), 69–91.

Young, M. D., Rodríguez, C., & Lee, P.-L. (2015). The role of trust in strengthening relationships between schools and Latino parents. *Journal of School Public Relations, 36*(4), 357–392. https://doi.org/10.3138jspr.36.4.357

Index

About the Author

Rosa L. Rivera-McCutchen is an associate professor of Leadership Studies at CUNY Lehman College, a Hispanic Serving Institution, where she also serves as the coordinator of School and District Leader certification programs. Rivera-McCutchen is also an affiliated faculty member in the Urban Education PhD Program at CUNY Graduate Center, and a faculty affiliate at the NYU Metropolitan Center for Research on Equity and the Transformation of Schools. An educator for over 20 years, she began her career as a high school teacher and advisor at Wings Academy in the Bronx before earning her doctorate in Teaching and Learning at New York University. A first-generation college graduate, Rivera-McCutchen's research, teaching, and activism is informed by her experiences attending and teaching in NYC public schools, and centers on achieving racial equity through radical care practices. She lives in New Rochelle, NY, with her husband, who is a public high school teacher, and their three children, who attend public schools.